HOW TO
FOOL
FISH
WITH
FEATHERS

Jon Margolis
Jeff MacNelly

A FIRESIDE BOOK
PUBLISHED BY SIMON & SCHUSTER
New York London Toronto Sydney Tokyo Singapore

Fireside
Simon & Schuster Building
Rockefeller Center
1230 Avenue of the Americas
New York, New York 10020

Library of Congress Cataloging-in-Publication Data

Margolis, Jon.
    How to fool fish with feathers : the incompleat guide to fly
fishing / by Jon Margolis and Jeff MacNelly.
        p.   cm
    1. Fly fishing. 2. Fly fishing—Humor. I. MacNelly, Jeff. II.
Title.
SH456.M28   1991   91-31737
799.1′2—dc20   CIP

Designed by Levavi & Levavi, Inc.

Manufactured in the United States of America

10   9   8   7   6   5   4   3   2   1

First Edition

ISBN 0-671-75943-4

Contents

INTRODUCTION

Question One: Why fly fishing?

Well, for one thing, it solves your problem if you don't like cleaning fish. You can't eviscerate what you can't catch.

No, let's try that again.

Question One (take two): Why fly fishing?

Contrary to what you may have heard and what was hinted above, it is possible to catch fish by fly fishing. It's just more difficult. Which is the point. You have to give the fish *some* advantage. After all, a trout, the principal (though not, as we will stress, the only) quarry of fly fishers, has a brain roughly the size of a pea. How can such a puny creature compete against this piece of work known as man? You want to know how? Try netting one with the use of only a few feathers wrapped around a tiny hook tied to a 12-foot-long, .007-inch-wide stretch of monofilament tied to a plastic line connected

The Good News:

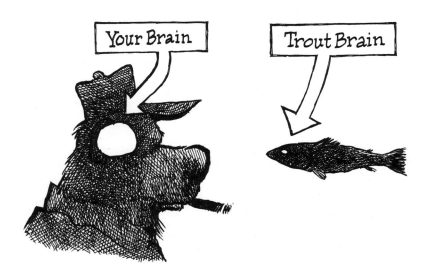

to an 8-foot-long graphite rod wielded by none other than yourself. You'll see how he can compete. Perhaps even this reply has not been entirely adequate. Let's try one more time.

Question One (take three): Why fly fishing?

Okay, seriously, this time, but we'll start by telling you why not. Not if your sole aim is catching fish, especially a lot of fish, especially a lot of big fish. All of which are fine aims *not to be abandoned by the would-be fly fisher*. Indeed, catching fish, many fish, using flies wet or dry is and must remain one of the things you want to do. And with just a bit of patience, effort, and luck, you will do it.

But note the wording. One of the things you want to do. Fly fishing is only for those who agree with this motto: "There

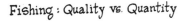

Fishing : Quality vs. Quantity

are two kinds of fishing, good fishing and great fishing. Great fishing is when you catch fish." Or as the Irish fisherman J. R. Harris wrote some fifty years ago, "The matter of importance is not so much how many fish are caught but rather how they are caught." Catching fish on a fly is harder, which means: (1) You won't catch as many, at least when you start; (2) you will at some point become frustrated and convinced that you will never even see or hook a fish, much less land one; and (3) when you do catch one (and you will, really you will), it's oh, so much more satisfying.

We will resist, until later, the temptation to wax too poetic about fly fishing, in large part because so many have so waxed so badly that it's hard to do it right anymore. But at the outset it must be said that there is a poetry to it, an artistry, and yes, even a mystery, and that if you doubt you are the type to connect to any or all of that, you might as well stop reading right now and return this to the bookstore shelf (assuming you are browsing; if you've already bought it, all we can say is: Thanks, and sorry, sucker.)

First of all, it's a great way to get outdoors, and usually in some very nice outdoors. As John Voelker (better known by

Good Fishing

his *nom de plume,* Robert Traver) put it, "There are no tele-
phones on trout waters." True, you will sometimes see anglers
casting their flies underneath the bridge of the interstate, but
far more frequently you won't see anyone casting flies at all,
because they're doing it far from where you can see it. Why
anyone would bother to fly fish beneath the interstate at all is
a riddle with which we will not attempt to deal, except to say
that it's sort of like seeking charm in a Ramada Inn. Fly fishing
is a contemplative pastime best pursued along streams and
lake shores and farm ponds where there are few cars going 20
miles an hour, much less 70, and not many people, either.

And yet, fly fishing is not just communing with nature and
getting away from it all. It's communing with nature and getting away from it all with a purpose in mind. Your purpose
is to catch fish. As much as any other activity, then, fly fishing
combines Eastern quiescence with Western dynamism. It is
both contemplative and active.

Second, there is something inherently creative about fly fish-

Great Fishing

ing. It requires, after all, what fishing philosopher Conrad Voss Bark called "the creation of an illusion," which might explain why fly fishing has appealed to so many writers. When you fish with live bait, you merely have to make sure that your bait gets to where a fish can see it. If he sees it, he'll try to eat it, assuming it's the right kind of bait for that kind of fish. If you use an artificial lure, you do have to fool the fish into thinking it's his food. You're engaging in deception. But deception is not quite the same thing as creating an illusion. In fly fishing, not only must you "fool" the fish into thinking that the wisp of rabbit fur and/or chicken feather you have placed on the water is the kind of bug he wants to eat, you also have to place it on (or sometimes in) the water so it behaves roughly the way a mayfly, grasshopper, or minnow would behave. And all that is just to get the fish to strike (never say bite) at your fly. Getting it into your net is another problem entirely. In fact, it's five or six other problems entirely.

And finally (for now, until we wax poetic later), fly fishing is a craft. It's not all that complicated or difficult a craft. In fact, it's not nearly as complicated or difficult as you have heard or as many fly fishing books would have you believe. But there is paraphernalia to be dealt with, some mechanics to be mastered, and an athletic skill (casting) to be learned. None of it is beyond the abilities of the normally (or even a touch less than normally) coordinated adult. (Children have far less trouble.) One need not be mechanically inclined. In fact, so simple are the mechanics that fly fishing provides a wonderful opportunity for even us clods to conquer mechanical problems, a great boon to the ego.

Actually, the paraphernalia, the athletic skill, and the mechanics are all part of the mystique. To enjoy fly fishing, you have to enjoy all of it, not just catching the fish. You have to regard putting on your waders and assembling your rod not as a pain in the neck but as part of the fun. You have not simply to tolerate but also to cherish the time spent taking the "memory" out of your leaders (explained presently). When you are standing in the middle of a stream, with trout rising around you and you have just lost your fly to an alder branch, you have to be happy, not frustrated as you find another fly and tie it on. True, you can't catch anything while you're twisting your tippet around the eye of a hook, but think of it this way: You're standing in the middle of a stream with an alder bush behind you and water gurgling all around you and perhaps a mountain range looming above. Besides, the fish will be in the water after your fly is tied on. In fact (assuming we can all do something about the acid rain), the fish will be in the water forever. So what's not to like?

If you think that's you, if you think you'd like standing in that stream, choosing which fly to use, luxuriating in the gurgle of the water, making sure to be a little more careful about that alder bush on the next backcast, knowing a little about tippets and lines and leaders and streamers and daces and Quill

Gordons and pale duns, then you're just the type to become a fly fisher.

Question Two: Who can fly fish?

Notice the use above of the term "fly fishers." Of yore, people spoke of "fly fishermen." That was in the unenlightened era. These days, some may speak of "fly fisherpersons." This is an awkward era. It is possible to be enlightened without committing aesthetic crimes.

The point is, fly fishing is a superb activity for women. The athleticism involved does not require brawn. Fly casting (an erroneous term, as we will presently demonstrate) is a matter of precision and coordination rather than brute strength, and while a day spent wading in swift waters can be pretty tiring for anyone, it is hardly beyond the abilities of women or of children over the age of, say, ten. The days when fly fishing was part of the male mystique are long gone. The day when fly fishing is a delightful activity, maybe even the second most delightful, for men and women to do together, is here.

Question Three: Is it expensive?

Kind of, but not nearly as expensive as you may have heard. Because many of the fly fishing instructors also work for tackle shops or equipment manufacturers, they have what the economists would call an incentive to convince you to buy a lot of fancy stuff. A fair amount of plain stuff will do to start.

A perfectly good rod can be bought, new, for not much more than $100. A simple, single-action reel is another $50, and both the reel and the rod should last for years. A fly line costs about $30, and no matter what anybody tells you, you only need one for now, probably a weight-forward floating line. Leaders cost about $2.50 apiece, and you should get about five of them. Flies are about a buck or $1.50 each, and while some will tell you that you need at least ten varieties,

Southern Summertime Waders

each in three- or four-hook sizes, you don't. Ten flies will be enough for openers.

Unfortunately, this is not all. You'll probably need waders. A pair of serviceable boot-foot chest waders cost about $50. Stocking-foot waders, which are easier to pack and carry, cost less, but then you have to buy a pair of wading boots, so the total price is higher. But if you are going to start out in shallow water, you can make do just fine with hip boots, which you can pick up in an Army-Navy store for twenty bucks or so. And here's something that purists will never tell you: If you are going to be fishing streams or ponds in south-

Stocking-foot waders and wading boots.

ern climes in summertime, you can wade right in with a pair of old sneakers and a bathing suit. You probably have them.

A vest ($40) is helpful, though probably not necessary for now. If you want to get a net, get a net. That shows a certain amount of confidence. But it's possible, even enjoyable, to land a fish without one. In other words, you can start for less than $400. Of course, if you have a friend willing to lend you some of his or her equipment to start, and to sell you some used equipment, your initial investment will be far lower.

Question Four: Why this book?

Because we're not experts. What follows is meant for the person who fears that he/she is a bit of a clod in these matters. We are not compleat (this is the Izaak Walton spelling) clods.

Waders

But we were. And not long ago, so we know what you need to know, and, perhaps even more important, we know what you don't need to know.

The trouble with experts, even those who write clearly, is that it's hard for them to remember that their readers are not. You know this if you've ever bought a computer, opened the instruction manual, and read something like, "Use the floppy disk drive to boot up the MS-DOS Operating System or to create a spreadsheet" when you haven't the foggiest idea what a floppy disk drive, MS-DOS, or spreadsheet are.

Similarly, a typical fly fishing book is likely to tell you something like, "First make a forehand knot and then insert the butt end of the leader inside the inner loop" before you know what a forehand knot or a butt end (of a leader, anyway) are supposed to be. We know you don't know. We know you're a compleat clod. (Actually, it's impossible to teach knot tying in a book, though we will make an effort in the Appendix. The important thing to remember is that you don't need to know how to tie all those knots.)

The standard fly fishing book, even for beginners, is likely to include an essay about different kinds of fly rods, with terms such as action and power-loading, none of which you need to know unless and until you decide to advance to the multirod stage. And the experts seem certain that you cannot venture into a stream without your entomology lesson complete with the life cycle of the Ephemeroptera (those are mayflies) and other information guaranteed to clog your brain and convince you that you'll never get the hang of this stuff. Actually, learning a bit about bugs (Did you remember before you read this paragraph that "entomology" is for bugs, "etymology" for words? Will you remember ten minutes hence?) and about pond and stream life in general are some of the sublime dividends of fly fishing. But you don't have to know all that much to start.

The other problem with experts is that they're so enthusiastic about fly fishing (for most of them it's their job, and they *should* be enthusiastic) that they think you'll be just as enthusiastic and spend scads and oodels of time learning how to tie knots, hitch leader butts to tippets, do the double haul, and figure out how to distinguish a Letort cricket from a fluttering caddis.

Here's what we know: You have a job, and maybe kids to drive to Little League practice or a lawn to mow or a book to read and several other things to do. One day, maybe, you'll be so enthusiastic about fly fishing that you'll learn all the esoterica. Now, you just want to learn the basics you need to get into that stream, cast your fly (as mentioned, the wrong term; you don't cast the fly, you cast the line) and maybe catch a fish. As we said at the outset, there is a mystique to fly fishing, and the mystique is part of the fun. But all the mysteries of the mystique need not be mastered to have the fun. At the stage you're at now, even at the stage you'd like to be at next year (hell, even at the stage *we're* at), fly fishing is a bit complicated, but it isn't all that complicated, and trying to get into too many of the complexities now is just confusing.

So we will try not to confuse. We will, however, try to amuse, another break with tradition. Your typical fly fishing expert is very, very serious. We are not. We hope you are not. If you are, get another book. Your typical fly fishing expert is single-mindedly interested in fly fishing. We'll throw in a few comments about our favorite and least favorite books, newspapers, politicians, and places to go. This is supposed to be fun, not school.

We have one more advantage. Because we work for a newspaper, we know how to be brief. Not so brief that you would confuse us with *USA Today,* which seems to think that all existence can be explained in four paragraphs. (Actually, you should not read *USA Today* lest you begin to write that way. Or worse, talk that way. As in, "Honey, I'm going to the store. Reason: We need a quart of milk." Or, "The living room needs vacuuming. Cited: dust under the couch.") No, working for a real newspaper, we know that existence needs sixteen to twenty paragraphs for full explication. The present exercise will be brief but adequate.

In these pages, we will tell you how to get your equipment, set it up, figure out where fish are likely to be, cast well enough so you can get your fly roughly where you want it, 35 or 40 feet away from you (which is all you'll need for now; we'll explain the double haul in Volume II), set your hook, land your fish, and have the time of your life. We'll also tell you a few places where you can go try your luck and your newfound skill. We'll continue doing it in the semi-Socratic method.

Oh, and one more thing: We're not snobs. Well, we're not such big snobs. Maybe you have to be a little bit of a snob to fly fish at all. But fly fishing is not just for trout in magnificent streams. We'll talk about bass, too. And you know what? You can fly fish for bluegills. In a farm pond. In fact, catching a bluegill on a two-weight or four-weight fly rod is a kick.

So sit back, relax, light up a cigar (you may not smoke them, but we do, and this is our book), and get ready to learn about something that can really (this is no joke) enrich your life for the rest of it.

1.

WHAT IT IS AND HOW YOU START

Just what is fly fishing?

A curse. No. It's a method of angling that uses a weightless artificial lure designed to fool a fish into thinking it's a natural bug, fish, or little animal.

How can it be weightless? Everything weighs something.

Oh, don't be pedantic. *We'll* be pedantic now and then. You're the pupil here. A little respect. Yes, as a law of physics, even a #22 midge weighs *something*. Let's say that it effectively weighs nothing.

If it (effectively) weighs nothing, how do you cast it?

You don't. Though we call it fly casting, you're casting the line. Unlike other fishing lines, fly lines are not thin stretches of monofilament. They are fairly thick strands of colored (usually green or yellow) plastic. They have weight.

If they're thick, how do you tie the fly to them?

You don't. You tie the fly to a leader, which *is* a thin strand of monofilament, very thin indeed at its tip, which is called (this shouldn't be too hard to remember) a tippet.

How do I tie the leader to the line? Is this one of these awful knots I have to learn?

Yes and no. There is a knot (see the Appendix), but thanks to a magnificent high-tech development, you don't have to learn it. This development is called a loop. Most fly lines these days come with a tough little loop tied onto the end. Most leaders come with the same. We bet that even you, you clod, can do the old loop-the-loop.

But doesn't this mess up that delicate presentation of the fly we have read about?

Technically, yes, and if you get to the point where you fish the Cheat or the Test or one of those still British chalk streams full of educated trout, you may want to learn the nail knot. But we have caught some very nice fish using looped lines and leaders.

How do we tie the fly onto the leader?

Technically, you tie the fly onto the tippet, which is the tiny tip of the leader. The top of the leader, up at the loop, is called the butt end, and is somewhat thicker, though you can hardly tell this with the naked eye. The leader gets thinner in stages. This is the one knot you really have to learn. But not yet.

Okay, how do we get started?

Go buy a fly rod. Buy one 8-foot-long graphite or boron rod built to hold a five-weight or six-weight line. Regardless

of what some purists say, any rod will also cast one up and one down. Meaning that your five-weight rod will also cast a four-weight and a six-weight line.

Eight feet? Isn't that kind of long and unwieldy?

Actually, it's a little on the short side. But, yes, it can be a little unwieldy, which is why we suggest it as a starter. You might even consider a 7½-footer.

Then what?

At the same time, and preferably at the same place, buy a reel, some backing, and one floating, weight-forward line to match your rod. Get the guy at the shop to put the backing and line on your reel. They don't charge for that; they're happy to have made the sale.

Don't these things ever come in sets?

Yes, and very often at a good price. A rod-reel-line combo might be your best bet. If you buy one of these sets off-season, when they're on sale, it can cost you about a hundred bucks.

It's that simple?

Not quite. Before rigging up your line, that guy at the shop (who could be a female guy these days) will ask you whether you reel with your left hand or your right. Traditionally, right-handed people reel with the left hand because you don't reel much in fly fishing; you strip in line with your free hand, and if you're a righty you'll want to hold the rod with your right hand. These days, more right-handers are opting to reel with their right hand. It's all very subjective.

Is that all we need?

Nope. You'll need some flys and a leader. Or better yet, for a few bucks more get one of these new leader kits. They come with a braided butt section that you pretty much just leave on your line, and a variety of tippet sections that you change as the weight of your fly changes.

Do these sections come with loops, too?

Oh, yes. That's the beauty part.

How many flies, and what kind?

As we said, about ten. Everybody should get a couple of muddler minnows (sizes 6 through 10) and a couple of royal coachmen or royal trudes (sizes 12 through 18). If you're going after trout in the East, get an Adams or two, small ones, a couple of Hendricksons in the size 12 through 16 range, and a somewhat larger LeTort Hopper. They work out

West, too. But you'll also want a few pale morning duns (16 or 18) for surface fishing and a slightly larger hare's ear for fishing below the surface. If bass is your prey, try a sneaky pete popper (size 8) or an even bigger hair mouse. Again, these are very general suggestions. Feel free to change them on the advice of your local tackle shop.

That's it?

Nope. Get a yarn rod.

What's that?

It's a wonderful, inexpensive little invention, a short, model fly rod with which you use some yarn in place of line and which you can use in your house to help you do the next thing you have to do, which is to learn the most important skill of all.

Which is?

Casting. We are now going to teach you how to cast.

2.

CASTING ABOUT

Okay, now we put the rod together, right?

Not indoors you don't. Remember, that's a long rod. If you try to go through the kitchen door with it, you might snap the end off. Take the rod, your reel, and a leader and head out to the backyard if you have one and it's big enough, to a park if not.

How big is big enough?

Well, you'll need some space. We're going to cast about 20 feet today, and remember this about casting: What happens in back is reversed in front, which means you'll need 20 feet behind you and 20 in front, with no low-hanging branches in between. Also, take this book and, if possible, a friend to read the instructions while you start casting.

Practice

Okay, we're outside. Now what?

Take the rod from its case or pouch. You have to put the two halves of the rod together (four if you bought a travel rod) by inserting the tip of the butt portion (that's the half with the cork near the bottom, beneath which you place the reel) into the bottom of the other portion. But don't do that just yet. First you want to put a touch of lubricant on the end of the butt half so you won't have to yank too hard when you take the rod apart later. That could cause damage.

Where's the lubricant?
Right on you.

On me?
Yup. Rub your finger alongside your nose, right where it meets the rest of your face. Even if you're the clean, well-groomed sort, there's a touch of oil there, sometimes used by pipe smokers to polish their pipe bowls. It's not much, but it's enough for our purposes. Just rub some around the tip of

The Butt End

The non-Butt, or Other End

Lubricating the Butt End

Lubricating with your nose

the bottom half of the rod, then insert that in the bottom of the other half. Now you're ready to put on your reel.

And how do we do that?

Simple. Hold the rod at the cork with the guides (those are the little rings through which you will string the line) pointing down. The reel, in case you didn't know, goes underneath the rod. Make sure the reel handle is on the side from which you're going to reel (remember, that's the left if you're a righty and a traditionalist). Turn the reel so the metal bar is facing up.

Now what?

Right at the base of the rod are three rings, two of which are not quite perfect circles, each having a little bump, creating

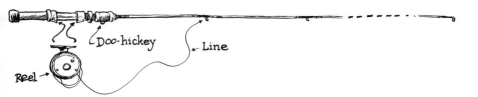

Reel

Doo-hickey

Line

a slot. One moves up and down; the other, closer to the base, doesn't. Some rods, especially smaller ones, vary the system slightly. They put the groove at the base of the cork handle, with the movable ring down at the base of the rod. Move the movable one up as high as it can go. Slip the back end of that metal bar on the reel into the slot in the unmovable ring. Then move the movable ring back down until it slips over the other end of the reel's metal bar and move the third ring (the one that is a perfect circle) right next to it and tighten it. You have now seated your reel and are ready to thread the line through the guides.

How do we do that?

Also pretty simple. Just pull the end of the line out. Holding the rod in one hand, slip the end of the line through each guide.

Including this little doohickey right on top of the cork?

No. That's to hook your fly into while you're walking from one spot where you caught no fish to another where your luck might change.

Okay, I've got it halfway up, and whoops! Oh, bleep. It fell back down.

Yup, that'll happen, and we purposely didn't give you one piece of advice there in order to make two points.

Which are?

One, that you'll say "Oh, bleep" a lot in this business. Two, to remind you that the line has weight and can easily slip back.

So how do we avoid that?

Strip out about three feet of line and double it, then pull it through that way, though the last guide is so tiny that you may have to do that one very carefully.

Now I have this thick green line hanging down here. Don't I need the leader?

Yes, but first you have to deal with the memory problem.

I haven't forgotten anything.

Not your memory problem. The leader's. The coiled mono-filament likes to stay coiled, even as you did after you left the womb. You have to take some of the memory out of it.

How do we do that?

Take the leader from this little packet, uncoil it, and then pull it through your thumb and forefinger several times. The heat will straighten it out.

Your Memory   Your Leader's Memory

Then what?

Loop the loop of the leader through the loop at the end of the line and pull the leader through. If you've bought one of those leader sets, you loop the loop of the thicker end of the braided butt through the line loop, then loop the loop of the tippet section through the other loop in the butt section. It's the same principle.

Great; now that's done. Don't we need a fly?

No, not for practice. If you want, you can tie one on, but we'd suggest that first you get a wire cutter and snap off the hook. This will lessen the chances that you will catch a leaf, your ear, or someone else's ear, with perhaps an ensuing lawsuit.

How do we tie it to the tippet?

Any old way you want, for now. When you get to the water, we'll teach you the knot.

So now we begin casting?

Well, for a minute or two, why don't you just stand there, get the feel of the rod, and try not to notice that your neighbor or the joggers running by in the park are looking at you as though you're some kind of nut. Just remember what the president said.

The president of what?

The United States. Though he was only a candidate then. But during the 1988 campaign, George Bush recounted "standing at the edge of the river, flipping my rod up and down with no effect." Somehow this never made the papers.

How do I hold the rod?

With your thumb on top of the cork grip, the thumbnail pointing straight toward the rod tip, and your fingers underneath the grip. The forefinger should do most of the gripping, with the other three fingers just kind of cradling the cork grip. Hold the rod parallel to the ground.

What do I do with my elbow?

Don't put it in your ear. Do keep it fairly close to your body. In the old days, they used to have young men hold either a Bible or a bottle of gin, depending on their priorities, against their bodies with their arms to keep their elbows close. But that was in the days of bamboo rods. These days you can let that elbow move out a bit, but not too far.

How do I stand?

On your feet, preferably. Put them as far apart as is comfortable, toes pointing forward. Now we're going to start.

How?

With your left hand (reverse all this if you're a lefty), strip just a little bit of line from the reel, and hold it in your left hand, about two feet diagonally to the left and in front of the reel, with the line lying on your forefinger and covered loosely by the thumb.

Okay, then what?

Lighten up on the thumb so it's really not holding the line, and flip the rod tip back and forth. What happens?

The line moves forward.

Right. Now pull just a little more line off and do that again, until you've got maybe 10 feet of line lying straight out in front of the rod.

I've got 10 feet out, but it's hardly straight.

Well, wiggle the rod up and down a little until the line straightens.

Done. Now what?

Now, keeping your elbow in the same place in relation to

your body, and *not snapping your wrist,* bring the rod tip straight up to the vertical. Not a miliblip farther. Do it as though the rod were an extension of your forearm.

The line went straight behind me and then flopped down.
Good; that's what it was supposed to do. Do it again.

Now what?
Again. Do it three or four more times. Make sure the rod tip moves in a straight line. Then, after that feels natural, we're going to make one little change.

What's that?
This time start bringing the rod tip up, and when you see your line lift entirely off the ground, increase the velocity of your arm movement *still without snapping your wrist,* still making sure the rod tip moves in a straight line, and still without bringing the rod tip any farther back than straight up. The aim here is for the forearm, wrist, hand, and rod to act as a unit. And don't bring the rod tip too far back.

Okay, I did it. That time the line stretched out straighter behind me.
Good. That's what it was supposed to do. Congratulations.

What for?
You just did the power snap. Keep doing it. Do it three or four more times, and look behind you. Remember to keep the rod tip moving in a straight line. Make sure that line stretches out straight. Don't let the rod tip go too far back.

Whoops. That time it didn't work right. The line flopped downward behind me.
That's because you brought the rod tip back too far, perhaps because you snapped your wrist back.

Isn't the wrist supposed to move at all?

Yes, but it does so naturally. In fact, if you've played baseball, golf, or tennis, your wrist, either from nature or culture, will tend to snap more than you want for fly casting. So we're intentionally exaggerating two points here, and one is to tell you not to snap your wrist at all.

What's the other?

Telling you not to bring the rod tip back any farther than straight overhead, or the twelve o'clock position. Most teachers will tell you to bring it back a little farther, to the one o'clock position. And they're right. But again, we know the tendency of beginners to snap back too far. So we start off by telling you twelve o'clock in the hope that you really will

stop it at one o'clock instead of bringing it all the way back
to five-thirty.

Makes sense. What's the next step?
This time, after your line stretches out straight behind you,
don't let it fall. Pause for just an instant after you see it
straighten, and then bring the rod tip forward in what is really
just an exact reversal of what you did to bring it backward.

Meaning?
Meaning to start just behind the vertical at about the one
o'clock position you've gotten to (because you couldn't stop
at twelve o'clock regardless of what we said). Bring the rod
forward in a straight line, without snapping your wrist. And
when the rod tip gets to about the twelve o'clock position,
increase the velocity of its movement (the power snap again)
*still without snapping the wrist, still moving that tip in a straight
line,* until you get to the ten o'clock position. Think of the
rod as a hammer and the imaginary spot in the air just above
the spot on the water where you want your fly to land as a
nail. Hammer that nail. Then you ease up, allowing the rod
to ease back to the horizontal, or nine o'clock position.

I don't follow through all the way down?
No. You don't power your rod to the water. You just stop
it and let it settle. You want your line to straighten out at
about 2 or 3 feet above the surface. Even at the end of the
your cast, *your rod tip should never dip below the horizontal.*

Okay, I did it.
Do it again. And again. And again.

Hey, my right wrist is beginning to hurt.
Not surprising, is it? Actually, that's probably enough for
today.

```
┌─────────────────────────────────┐
│  Very Small Things:             │
│                                 │
│    ∘ HEAD OF PIN                │
│    • QUARK                      │
│    ∘ BRAIN OF TROUT             │
│                                 │
└─────────────────────────────────┘
```

You mean I know how to cast?

You know how. But you still can't do it. You're making about twelve different mistakes, but we'll work on that next time.

Tomorrow?

No, the day after tomorrow. Tomorrow, work with the yarn rod.

Oh, the yarn rod. How does that work?

Take 12 feet of yarn and string it through the rod as though it were fly line. Take some shoe polish and make marks 2, 4, 6, 8, and 10 feet from the start of the line. Tomorrow evening, let about 4 feet of yarn out from the rod tip, sit in your favorite chair, and do some mock casting. Remember to keep your wrist firm and the tip moving in a straight line. Remember not to bring the rod too far back, to let it stretch out behind you before you start the forward cast, and to stop it at the vertical. Remember when to start and when to stop the power snap.

Wow. Anything else to remember?

Yes, remember not to get all atizzy. You're having fun, right?

3.

CASTING ABOUT INDOORS

Now we can go out again?

Not for a few days. First we're going to stay in for a while. We'll work with the yarn rod for a day, then we'll go to the backyard one more time.

WRONG.

Okay, I've got the yarn rod, with black blobs at the right places. Now what?

Get the cat out of the room.

The cat?

Yeah. Cats just love to play with yarn. You can't work with your yarn rod if a cat is around.

Okay, she's in the other room. But she is not pleased. Now what do I do?

Sit down.

Sit down?

Sure. In fact, you might want to sit on the floor. Even though that yarn rod is only 3 feet long, 3 plus 6 feet of yarn plus the length of your arm are probably more feet than your ceiling is high unless you've restored one of those old Victorian jobs.

All right. I'm down. Now what do I do?

First of all, remember to stay flexible. Especially remember to keep your neck loose. You'll want to follow the tip of the yarn with your eyes, even at the start, when all you'll do is make circles.

Circles?

Yup. Put the 6-foot mark at the tip of the rod and hold the rest of it crumpled up in your rod hand, scrooched against the handle.

Scrooched?

Listen. It's our book. We make up our words.

Fair enough. What do I do with my other hand?

Forget about it for now. Just take the rod and make circles with it.

Right.

What kind of circles?

Big ones. Keep your wrist straight, keep your elbow bent and pretty close to your body, and make big circles with your arm. Nothing subtle here. Don't let the yarn tip fall. Keep it moving continuously, and keep your eye on it.

This isn't too difficult.

No, it isn't. Now try figure eights, or ovals, or some other doodaddery. Just keep it moving for a few minutes.

This is kind of boring.

Right. Okay, now stop. Bring the rod to your waist, hold the rod parallel to the floor, and move the yarn tip from side to side.

All the way back and forth like that?

No, just move it about a foot to the right and then bring it back till it goes about a foot to the left. Remember, keep your arm straight and your wrist stiff.

Okay, got it.

Good. Now, on the next stroke, stop the cast *very abruptly* and see what happens.

The yarn just unrolled to its full length, and then it fell.

Right. Next time, though, don't let it fall. As soon as it rolls all the way out, snap it back the other way.

Hey, this is kind of fun.

Good. Now, on your next cast to the left, allow the yarn to straighten out, and then follow it down by lowering the rod.

It landed, but kind of wrinkled.

That's because you didn't lower the rod quite fast enough. Keep trying it until the yarn lands straight out. It just takes a little practice.

Now I've got it. Is that all there is to it?

Pretty much. But we're going to get a little more elaborate. Go get a couple of books and put them on the floor, each book about 6 feet from you, one to the right and one to the left.

Done. Now what?
Now you do pretty much the same thing you just did and see how close your yarntip comes to the books.

Not very, that time. It just plopped down too early.
That's because your hand was jumping all over the place instead of staying parallel to the floor.

That was better, but it didn't quite get all the way there.
That's because you pulled up too early and didn't follow through.

I thought we weren't supposed to follow through.
Well, we sort of lied.

You can't "sort of" lie. That's like being a little pregnant.
Don't philosophize. We're the teachers here. In fly casting, one of the big problems is too much follow-through. So we told you not to do it at all. You don't want to follow through the way you do serving in tennis or batting in baseball. But you do want to follow the linetip down by lowering the rod just after you complete the forward power move. We'll explain this more when we go back outdoors.

Are we ready to do that yet?
Not quite. So far, you've just done the yarn rod from side to side. Now you've got to do it overhead.

Oh, you mean like real casting?
Yes, though on small streams or in places with lots of growth overhead you'll find yourself casting sidearm quite a bit. But now, do what you've been doing with the yarn rod, but move to the vertical. Not all at once, but by changing the

plane a few inches at a time, keeping the line in motion. In other words, do up and down what you've been doing back and forth.

Just like real casting.

Yes, with this one exception: Don't bring the rod back next to your shoulder. Bring the rod right up to your face, so that at the end of your backcast your hand is right between your eyes, though maybe a touch higher.

Why?

So you'll get that sharp, snappy action, in preference to cold-cocking yourself, which experience hath shown most people would rather avoid. Also, you can see more easily just what you might be doing wrong. In the long run, we can help, but you have to teach yourself.

All right. I think I'm doing it right. I'm hitting those books most of the time.

Yes, you are. Now try doing it on every snap, with no false casting.

Is that it?

Pretty much. But now get fancy. Try going from one plane to another without stopping. Pick out a whole bunch of targets and try hitting them all. Move around if you can. Hit the lamp next to the couch. Hit the cat if she has come back into the room, and snap it away before she can grab it. Hit the woofer knob on the stereo, the top branch of that absurd plant near your window, the candlestick on the dining room table. Keep moving, keep your wrist straight, keep that arm and the rod moving as though they are one.

You know, not only is this kind of fun, it's also pretty.

Yes, it is, isn't it.

4.

SUITING UP

Are we going out to the backyard again?

No. You've done enough of the ersatz. It's time to go to the water.

You mean we're actually going fishing?

Well, for now let's just say that we're going to practice casting in a real stream.

Great. I've got my rod, my reel, my line, my leader, and my nose, I'm all prepared.

Your nose?

Yeah, you know, for the oil to put the rod together. Just wanted to show you how much I remembered. Anyway, I'm all ready.

No, you're not.

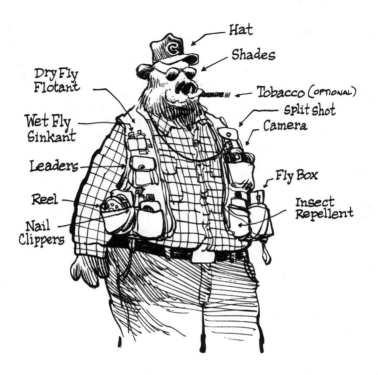

Hat

Shades

Dry Fly
Flotant

Tobacco (OPTIONAL)

Split Shot

Camera

Wet Fly
Sinkant

Leaders

Fly Box

Reel

Insect
Repellent

Nail
Clippers

No? What else do I need?

For one thing, you'll need a fly. This time we're going to cast real flies. Remember, you bought a few of them, and they're in a little fly box.

Yup. Got 'em right here. What else?

Your boots or waders. We're going into the water.

Why? Don't the fish come close enough to shore?

Oh, they're often very close to shore. But in most places, if you try to backcast from shore, you'll catch a lot of branches, not to mention a few rocks, and perhaps another fisher. In fact, you'll catch enough of them casting from the water. But fewer.

Oh, I see. Well, good. Because, you know, I bought these things, but I'm not quite sure how they work. I bought both, actually, boots and waders. But they're kind of confusing.

Indeed they are. And one problem is that the confusions are so elementary that most beginners are embarrassed to ask just what all these little hooks and straps are for.

Yeah. For instance, on these hip boots. What are these little lace things down in the actual boot part?

Well, they're to lace up, if you want to. Frankly, though, it's hardly worth trying to stick your hands down into the boot to do it. It's kind of a waste of time.

I thought as much. Now, what about these straps up here at the top, near the top of my leg?

You'll notice there are two of them. One, that goes horizontally, fits into that buckle to tighten the boot top against your leg. The other one you loop through the belt of your pants, or the belt loops, if you're not wearing a belt, then snap it on that snap there. That keeps the boot up.

Oh. Now that you've explained it, it seems so simple. But tell me one more thing: These boots come up near the top of my thigh, not to my hips. Why are they called hip boots?

This is one of the great mysteries. Let's get to the stocking-foot wader.

Yes, let's. I tried them on once, but I put them on backward.

A common error. Take them out of their little case and hold them up. You'll see metal buttons. They're for hooking on the suspenders, and you'll note that there are more of them on one side than on the other.

So?

So the side with more is the front. The suspenders have two buttonholes on each front strap, but only one for each strap in the rear.

Aha. Now what about these funny, socklike things the guy at the store told me I absolutely had to have?

"Absolutely had to" was a bit of an exaggeration. But not much of one. They're special neoprene socks that keep the sand and grit of the stream from getting inside your boot.

Well, do I put them on under the waders or over?

Over. First, put wool socks on over your street socks.

Wool socks on a hot day like this?

If that stream holds trout, it's cold water. If the socks have elastic around the top, and I hope they do, tuck your pants into them. That makes it less likely that your pants will start riding up during the course of the day.

Ah, I see. Okay. Then put the waders on over the wool socks?

Right.

Okay, Now I've got them on the right way, and I put on these suspenders. Wow! This is as big a pain as putting on a tuxedo.

Exactly. But what you do after you've got them on is a lot more fun.

Next come the neoprene socks?

Right. And then the boots. I hope you got them big enough to fit over the neoprenes.

Yes, I tried them on that way.

Good.

Now, I'm lacing these boots, and they seem to come with some little ball thing through the laces. Does it serve any purpose?

No.

Great, I'm all set.

Not until you fold the tops of the neoprene socks down

over the boot tops. Otherwise their debris-guarding function will be for naught.

Okay. Here I am. Do I look like a fisherman?
Nope. You forgot the belt.

Oh, yeah. This little black belt came with the waders. Do I really need it?
Really need? No. But if you do fall in, it will help keep water out of your waders.

There. I'm belted. Now do I look like a fisherman?
Not quite, though you're getting there. Did you get a vest?

Yeah. It's got as many pockets as one of those vests news photographers use.
It *is* one of those vests news photographers use.

Oh. What goes where?
Well, for now put your reel in one of the bigger pockets on the right side, your leaders in another, and your fly box in one of the pockets on the other side. Basically, vest organization is very subjective. And you'll forget where you've put what you want half the time anyway. Most fly fishers spend hours every day searching through their vest pockets.

Done. Do I need anything else?
Just a few little things. You'll need either a silicone compound known as "flotant" in the trade to help keep your dry flies dry, and therefore floating, or wet fly sinking stuff to help keep your wet flies and streamers *from* floating. Better take one of each. You never know what the fishing situation will be.

Oh, yeah. I bought those, too. What else?
Better get some insect repellent and slip it in one of the

little pockets up near the top of the vest. And then remember to bring one of the most valuable of all a fly fisher's tools.

Which is?

Nail clippers. Best to clip them somehow to the outside of the vest, attaching the clippers to one of those rings you see on the vest.

What about a net and a creel?

A net can't hurt. Get one with a doohickey you can hook into a ring which ought to be on the back of your vest.

Voilà! The vest. Now I look like a fisherman.

No, you don't.

Still no, huh?

Afraid so. First of all, you're bareheaded. If the sun is shining, it will shine from both above and off the water below. You'll want a cap. Also sunglasses. Preferably Polaroids.

What kind of hat?

Again, it's your call. But a simple baseball cap will do, preferably with the insignia of either a ball club or a farm implement manufacturer. At the outset, you don't want to put on airs.

Voilà again! *Mon chapeau. Et mes spectacles de soleil.* Now do I look like a fisherman?

You do. And you know what that proves?

No. What?

Appearances can be deceiving. Let's go to the water.

Absolutely <u>not</u>

not yet...

Perfect

5.

DOWN BY
THE RIVERSIDE

Wow! There it is! The river! Let's fish.

Well, okay. But let's not get carried away. This is a good opportunity to review. First, we suit up.

Right. Woolen socks over the street socks, tuck in the pants. More wader buttons in front. Neoprene socks over the waders. Boots on. Fold down the neoprenes. Don't forget the belt. Hat. Glasses. Vest. How'm I doing?

Just fine, Mayor Koch. Now we rig up.

Right again. Lubricate the rod fittings. Fit the reel on. Double the line to feed it through the guides. Take the memory out of the leader. Loop the leader to the line. Whoops. This time, you say, we're going to use a real fly?

Yup. And for now, we'll just use the simplest of all dry flies, a #14 Royal Coachman.

What's that?
It's the red thing with the white wings right here in your fly box.

What kind of real fly does it imitate?
No kind.

No kind?
No. Considering that we don't really know this stream, what may be hatching here, what naturals the fish are eating at this time of day and this time of year, we're just going to try an attractor.

An attractor?
Yes. We'll go into this in a little more detail when we discuss fly selection. But sometimes it's good enough just to use something that will catch the fish's eye, especially when you don't know what's going on. That's an attractor. And there's none better than the old coachman.

Well, here it is. How do I tie it on?
Simple. You've got your leader looped to your fly line. Now get the tiny end of the leader, the tippet, in one hand, and hold the fly in the other. Hold it so your fingers don't cover up the eye.

The eye?
Yes. Just like a needle. The little circle through which you put the tippet.

Oh. Say, this tippet is tiny. It's hard to find the end.
You think that's tiny. Because we're using a size 14 fly, sort

of midsize, that's a 3X tippet. We could have used a 4X, too. There's a formula for figuring out what size leader to use.

A formula?

Yes. The fly size should be four times the tippet size. So a size 16 fly takes a 4X leader, a 12 takes a 3X. Our size 14 here is in the middle, and to make life easier we'll go with the 3X. But when you start fishing 20s and 22s, you'll be using 5x and even 6x leader. Those tippets are hard to see.

Well, now I have it, and I'll just put it through the eye of this . . . Hey, this is hard. It's like threading a needle.

Exactly.

But I've got it. Now what?

This is the only knot we're really going to teach you, though we'll explain a few others at the end. This is called the clinch knot, and it's so simple that even you can do it.

How?

First, pull about 6 inches of the tippet through the eye. Then, holding the fly with one hand and the leader with the other, loop the end of the tippet (the part that's been pulled through the eye) around the part of the tippet just in front of the eye five times.

Done. Now what?

Right up at the fingers holding the fly, you have created a little loop. See it?

Little is right.

Big enough. Stick the end of the tippet through that loop. But don't pull it tight yet.

It's through.

Good. Now pull it slowly, but just before it gets tight, moisten the knot a little with your mouth. Then pull it tight.

Is that all?

Well, we usually hold the fly in one hand and hold the leader about 18 inches up and yank to see if it's holding.

It's holding, all right. But what do I do with the leftover tippet end that's sort of hanging down here?

Take that all-purpose tool, the nail clipper, and clip it off, taking care not to clip the wrong strand, the one the fly is tied to.

How dumb do you think I am?

About as dumb as every other fly fisher. Everybody does it now and then. When you've clipped it off, give it the old yank test again.

It's on.

Good, but let's do one more thing.

What's that?

Take your forceps or some kind of pliar-type tool and pinch down the barb of the hook.

Won't that make it harder to keep a fish if I get one?

Not much. And it makes it much easier to unhook him without hurting him.

Okay. Done.

Good. We will now head down to the stream.

Hey, it's *weird* walking in these boots.

So it is. You'll get used to it. Okay, here's the water. The only way to get into it is to get into it.

Oh, boy! Here I go. *Hey,* it's slippery!

Water does that. We've gone in at a spot where the river bottom is pebbly, which makes it a bit slippery. Wading can be tricky, even dangerous. Fortunately, this stream is shallow and not too swift right here. That's why we chose this spot. It's a good idea to get the hang of it where it isn't too difficult. Even in these conditions, though, it's best to wade slowly. Try to see where you're putting down your foot with each step. If you can't see, feel your way with your foot. You wouldn't want to step into a deep hole.

No, but I have another problem.

What's that?

I think my waders are leaking.

What makes you think that?

My feet and lower legs are cold.

That doesn't mean you have a leak. The water is cold. Unless you have neoprene waders, which you only need if you do a lot of fishing in very cold water, it's going to be cool. If you're uncomfortable, next time you might try wearing long johns. But you'll be fine once you get used to it. Now, let's walk right over to this shallow, pebbly spot and practice casting right over there near the bank, where it's a little deeper.

Why there?

There might actually be fish there.

Okay, we're here. Now, are we going to review our casting lesson?

Right. Stand comfortably, toes pointing forward. Strip a few feet of line from the reel and hold it in your left hand. Now start flipping the rod back and forth.

Right. I remember. Now I strip a little more line out, right?

Right again. Now bring the rod tip up, power it back, look

behind you, and when you see it straighten out behind, bring it forward, but remember, not too far forward. Keep it from ten o'clock to one o'clock. Really to noon, until you get more experience.

There. I'm doing it. I'm doing it. Now I'll try a real cast. I'll hit that spot in the pool just under that tree, and I'll . . . *Hey!* What's going on?

What's going on is that you have caught a very fine alder branch on the bank about 20 feet behind you. Don't despair. It's every fly fisher's first catch.

What happened?

You brought the rod tip too far back. I think you snapped your wrist too much on the backstroke, too.

Okay, now what do I do?

You walk back there, slowly, and unhook the branch. Think of it as getting more wading practice.

Here I go again. Now I'm getting it. Watch this. Well, I didn't catch a branch, but the line fell right in front of me.

Yup. You started your forward cast too soon.

Yes, I did. Now I'll do it. Well, I got to sort of the right place, but the leader kind of bunched up around the fly. That's not good, is it?

No. For one thing, you won't get much accuracy that way. For another, should a fish take your fly, you'll have far too much slack in the line and leader to be able to set the hook. You want that line and leader to be stretched out to their full length as much as possible.

What did I do wrong there?

You didn't use any power. Remember the hammer and nail analogy. Drive that nail. Wait until the line straightens out

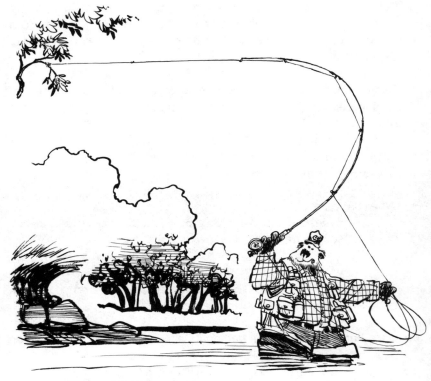

Every Fly Fisherman's First Catch

behind you, maybe wait one more second, and then bring it forward, and when you get back to about the eleven o'clock position, drive that nail.

Okay, here we go again. This time I'll . . . *Hey! Bleep blap bleep it!* I got that alder branch again. What do I do now?

   Walk back there. Unhook that branch. And realize that you'll say bleep blap bleep it a lot in this business.

All right, now I'm really determined. I'm going to watch my back-cast. I'm going to bring it forward. I'm going to drive that nail. And there we are. That fly is heading right to that pool. Look at that. *It's* there. It's drifting down with the current. It's . . . *Hey!* What was that?

That was a fish.

A *fish?*

Yup. A fish took your fly. But since you didn't know it, you didn't set the hook.

Oh, no. And now I've scared him. I'll never get him.

Not so. Wait about two minutes. Dry your fly off with a few false casts and try again.

It was hardly noticeable. It was the tiniest little flash of silver, a delicate splash, and the gentlest of tugs on my line. Is it always like that?

Often.

What do I do if he takes it again?

Set the hook.

How do I do that?

Just a quick, firm (but gentle) lifting of the rod. And then keep that rod tip up. If there's slack in the line, he'll throw the hook.

Oh, it was wonderful. Now I'm going to try again. Backcast, bring it forward, drive that nail. Hey, I got to the same spot. Now it's drifting down. Now. *There it is. And I've got him. I did it! I did it!* Now I know how to fish.

Well, in a sense, now your troubles are just beginning.

6.

OMIGOD, I'VE CAUGHT A FISH

Now what do I do?
Several things all at once. And all very quickly.

Now he tells me. Where do I start?
Keep your rod tip up.

All the way up?
Pretty far up. Between ten and eleven o'clock.

There you go with the clocks again.
Almost vertical, if you don't like clock talk. But never beyond the vertical.

Beyond the vertical?
That is to say, the rod tip should never be pointing *away*

from the fish, even for a second. But we don't have time right now to palaver.

No, that baby is flipping around down there like a madman.

That's what they do. I assume you're holding the line tight against the rod with the forefinger of your right hand.

You do? Well, what do you know? I am. Why did you assume that?

Because otherwise that little fish you've got there would probably have shaken the hook right out of his little mouth. I can see that your left hand is nowhere near the line.

Oh. Right. It isn't. Was that a mistake? And how do you know it's a little fish?

Yes, it was a mistake. You always need line control. You never know when a fish will hit. Get the line in your left hand, but hold it gently, with your thumb on one side and your index and middle fingers on the other, loose enough so that if the fish pulls on it, the line will slide through. Same with the forefinger of your right hand. Keep it loose. Right now. You've got the line locked against the rod, which is why I know it's a little fish. A big one would have broken off your tippet by now.

So you mean I have to keep the line taut, with no slack in it, but loose at the same time?

Exactly.

That's a bit tricky, isn't it?

This is all a bit tricky. Keep that rod tip up.

Okay. And by the way, what's the difference between a forefinger and an index finger?

Nothing, dummy. It's the same thing.

Oh. Well, he's still flipping around down there in the water. Now what do I do?

Start stripping in.

How?

Since he's not very big and not very far away, just strip in line with your left hand, but gently.

Okay, I'm doing it. Hey, this is fun. This is more than fun. This is downright exhilarating.

Yes, it is. Keep that rod tip up. And keep stripping gently. If he wants to swim away and seems able to do so, let him. When a fish wants to take line, you give him line.

Always?

Pretty much. Though if he's going to head toward a patch of weeds or a log where he can wrap the leader around something and break off the tippet, then you have to move to try to steer him away from those obstacles. But we don't have any of those around here, which is one reason we chose this little stretch of stream to start with. Keep that rod tip up.

Okay, I've got him a little closer now. He's still flipping around as though his life depended on it.

Well, as far as he's concerned, it does. He doesn't know you plan to release him. He doesn't know anything, except that all of a sudden he can't swim where he chooses. Keep that rod tip up.

You're really obsessed by this rod tip, aren't you?

No double entendres, please. But yes, and for good reason. It has to become second nature, so we're drilling it into you, sort of like irregular verbs: Keep the rod tip up, keep the line taut, give the fish line if he takes it.

Okay. I've just about got him now. A few more strips and I'll . . .

Keep that rod tip up.

Oh. Right. Now I'll strip in and . . . wait. Is he gone? I think he's gone.

He's gone.

What happened?

You let the rod tip down too low, which left slack in the line, and he threw the hook.

It was down for only a second.

That's all it takes. Trout (and that was probably a trout; though it could have been a small panfish) have small, delicate mouths, and they often sip those bugs (as he assumed it was) very gently. In many cases, they're hooked quite tentatively, and if that line isn't holding the hook in there very tightly, they can throw it.

Oh. Well, I've failed. It's kind of confusing keeping all that in mind at once. Stripping, keeping the line taut but loose, holding the rod tip up.

Yes, it is, and yes, you have failed. But don't let it get you down: As we said at the start, there's much more failure than success in fly fishing, which is what makes success all the sweeter. We all lose fish. Even the real experts. There are more of them down there, though.

More real experts?

No, more fish.

Well, should I try again?

Let's pause for a little discussion first, and let us ask you a question: How did you know you had that fish on your hook?

You know, that's a very good question. I'm not really sure. How does one know?

Ah-hah! Here's one of the wonderful mysteries of fly fishing. You often don't.

You don't know when a fish is hooked?

Sometimes you don't know. And even more often you don't know why you know. Sometimes you see it and sometimes you feel it. But more often you sort of see it and sort of feel it at the same time. A little flip of fin or stirring of the water, plus a barely perceptible tug on the line. Either way, you set the hook. So we'll ask you another question: How did you set the hook?

Well, you told me what to do, but I'm not sure I did it.

Neither are we. We think that baby sort of hooked himself for you. A little piece of luck that happens from time to time. But not often. Usually you have to do it yourself. So we'll start there. The first two challenges are knowing when you have a strike and setting the hook.

Fine. What are the secrets?

There are none. But the best answer is that any time you think you *might* even have a strike, set the hook by keeping that line pinched against the rod with the index finger of your rod hand and raising the rod tip, firmly but not too hard.

Oh, another one of your balancing acts?

Exactly. If you go fishing with experienced fly fishers and you try to set the hook with a great big yank, two things will ensue.

Which are?

The fly will come shooting right back at you with nothing attached to it. And you will get a good deal of comment about how you have reversed the fish's oral and anal orifi, no doubt expressed in less scientific terms.

Let me go back a minute to this business of thinking I might even have a strike. What do you mean by that?

Especially for beginners, it's often hard to know, and lots

of people miss catching fish because they don't know that one has hit their fly.

So what's the solution?

Strike at any possibility. The worst thing that will happen if you don't have a strike is that you'll yank your fly back toward you. If that happens, try to make it the start of your backcast, preferably doing this so smoothly that anyone else who's around won't even know that you've just tried to set the hook because your fly swirled around in an eddy for a second. Then you just cast again. But if you see a fish rise to your fly, or even just see a swirling in the water where your fly is, set the hook.

Well, that brings up another question. I often couldn't see my fly. Maybe my eyesight isn't good enough.

No. None of us can always see our fly. Quite often, what you think is your fly is a real bug on the water, or just some swirling foam. But you usually have a pretty good idea of roughly where it is. You can almost always see the end of your fly line, and if you know how long your leader is, you can figure out roughly where your fly ought to be. If anything happens in that general area, set the hook.

Okay. By pinching the line tight and raising the rod tip firmly but not too hard, right?

Right, although none of this applies to bass, which we'll deal with later. Also, if the fish hits your fly straight downstream from you, move the rod sideways instead of up.

I can probably remember that. Then what do I do?

Then it depends on the size of the fish, which you can usually feel pretty well. If he (or, as often as not, she; but it makes no difference) can take line, give him line.

And let him go wherever he wants?

Well, not entirely. In addition to keeping him away from

weeds and branches, it's best to keep him upstream from you, so you're not fighting the current as well as the fish. But if the current isn't strong, that's not too much of a problem.

Then what?

Keeping that rod tip up, at between ten and eleven o'clock, strip in when he's not insisting on line. (Later, when we talk about bigger fish, we'll deal with playing them from the reel.) Don't let him rest. This is for his sake as well as yours.

How's that?

If you're going to release the fish, the less time he's fighting that line, the more likely he is to survive.

Makes sense. But what about if he jumps. What do I do then?

Commit heresy.

What heresy?

Lower the rod tip.

Lower it?

Yes. The salmon fishermen call it "bowing." In the air, a fish is effectively a lot heavier than in the water. Even a vigorous shaking of his head while he's aloft can snap off a taut tippet. In this case, slack is your friend.

Ah, I see. But then as soon as he's back in the water, get that rod tip up again?

Exactly.

And how do I know when I can really bring him in.

A fish is usually played out when he stops thrashing and starts swimming in tight circles. When he does that, strip him as close to you as possible. But be careful of one thing.

Fish Up–Rod tip Down

What's that?

When he sees you, he'll panic and maybe try to make one more run. But by then he's pretty well tuckered out.

And when he's right near me.

Don't do what so many beginners do and move your hand from the butt of the rod. Move the rod away from your body and guide the fish as close to you as possible.

Then what?

Hold the rod, keeping the line taut with that index finger, and get your net from wherever you keep it (make sure it's hooked or strapped to you so you can do this quickly).

Great. And then just scoop him up with the net, right?

Wrong. Put the net into the water and guide the fish above it. Then raise the net from under the fish.

Is that it?

Just about. Why don't you try again.

Where?

The same place you hooked that fish before. You might get him again.

Won't he be wary now?

No, we've given him enough time. And he's only a fish. Cognition is not his strong suit.

Okay, here I go. No, nothing that time.

Cast a bit upstream and let the fly drift over the spot where he was.

Here I go again, this time with line control. It's upstream, it's drifting down, it's . . . there's something, I'm setting the hook. *I've got him!*

Good. Keep the rod tip up, keep line control, and strip in as quickly as you can.

All the way?

No, you want to make sure that you don't strip the leader up to the rod. When the loop joining your line and leader gets to the rod tip, don't strip any more. But you're not there yet, so keep stripping.

I am. I am. I see him. He's not too big, but not that small, either. Wait, he's pulling on the line. I'm giving him line.

Good.

Now he stopped again, and I'm stripping in line, and, *wow!* There he goes. He's jumping. And I'm bowing the rod tip, and now he's back in the water and my rod tip is up again.

Good work. He's not all that tiny. Looks like an 8-incher.

Is that big?

No. It's small, but it's a real fish. Not a tiny one.

All right. Now he's closer. Good Lord, this is fun. I remember what you said. Hold the rod in my right hand, grab my net with my . . . oof, there it is. Bring him in, put the net under the water, guide the fish over it, raise the net, and *there he is. My first fish.* This is wonderful. Look. Here he is. Right in my net. I'm a success.

Good, but there's one more thing to learn.

What's that?

How to release him.

Right. How do I do that?

First, always wet your hands before you touch a fish. Then, see if you can just grab the fly and twist it out of his mouth without touching him.

I think I can. He's just hooked at the corner of the lip. And I did remember to pinch the barb of the hook down, so it shouldn't be too hard. There. It's out. Now I just dump him back in the water?

No. Lift him out of the net very gently, by cupping your fingers under his belly and scooping him up.

Got him. Then what?

Hold him in the water, his head facing upstream so the water can wash over his gills and he can get oxygen. Hold him until he starts wiggling his tail. Then just open your hand to release him.

Done. Goodbye, my friend.

Oh, you'll do fine.

Why do you say that?

Because you knew he was your friend.

He was. And he was pretty.

Yes, he was.

So that's it? I'm done learning? I'm a success?

Oh, you're only a very limited success.

How's that?

You're a success if all you want to do is catch an occasional small fish. If you want to catch a lot, and catch bigger ones, you've still got a lot to learn.

Such as?

Such as how to land a fish when your tippet is really tiny; that 3X you had on is clothesline compared to the 6X or 7X you have to use sometimes. And how to figure out where the fish are more likely to be instead of just getting lucky. And how to make it far more likely that you'll attract a fish who has alternatives, as opposed to this guy, who just happened to see your attracter fly when not much else was going past, which is often the case in the middle of the day.

Oh. I guess you're right. Actually, though, it's not really the middle of the day anymore.

No, twilight is coming. Break down your rod and we'll head home.

Okay, that's done. Now it's getting dark. Good heavens, look at all these bugs flying around. There must be a million of them.

At least.

It's a veritable swarm.

No, it's a veritable hatch.

Oh, yeah. A hatch. Why is it called a hatch?

Because that's what they all just did.

What did they just did?

They hatched. Which is the subject of the next chapter.

7.

OF FLIES AND FLIES
OR
THE ETYMOLOGY
OF THE ENTOMOLOGY

Now what is all this about hatches?

Let's go over a few basics. Fly fishing involves the creation of an illusion. Usually that illusion concerns bugs, the kind that live most of their lives in and on the water. Later we'll get into creating the illusions of minnows and other tiny fish, and even of frogs and mice. But for now we're dealing with bugs (though a biologist would call them insects, not bugs), and there are two good reasons to learn a little bit about them.

And they are?

Reason one is that it helps us catch more fish, and bigger ones, too. In fact, sometimes it's the only way, as well as the most exciting way, to catch fish. Reason two is that it's kind of fun.

When is it the only way?

When there's a real hatch on. When you approach a stream and the air is full of insects that have just hatched, it's a pretty good bet that only one kind of fly is hatching, and that it is the only kind of fly the fish are eating. And when the air is full of them, soon the water will be full of them, too, and the fish will be feeding like crazy. Sometimes the water seems almost to be boiling, so many fish are rising, slurping, and splashing. It's a fly fisher's nirvana.

All right. But at the beginning, you said we wouldn't have to get into all the minutiae and learn how to identify all these insects. After all, a bug is a bug is a bug.

Well, not quite. How about somewhere between becoming an entomologist and dismissing it all as a bug is a bug is a bug? Bugs aren't roses. Furthermore, there are different kinds of roses, and anyway, Gertrude Stein didn't know bupkis about fishing.

Well, okay. But do we have to learn all those fancy names?

You mean like Ephemeroptera and Tridelphia and Altacocktera and all that? No. There are something like 20 skillion kinds of mayflies alone, and even some of the professional entomologists can't agree on all the taxonomy.

Taxonomy?

No, this has nothing to do with your 1040. That's the fancy word for plant and animal classification. It's another word we can forget. Besides, there's a difference between what scientists call some flies and what fishers call them.

For instance?

Well, for instance, on the upper Missouri in midsummer, on most mornings there's something called a trico hatch, which is what the locals call the particular kind of caddis fly, perhaps because the scientific name for the caddis—all caddises, and there are many species—is Trichoptera. But the fly you want for this is not called a caddis or a Trichoptera. It's an Adams parachute or something called a house and lots.

How do you know that?
Through the time-honored scientific method of asking the folks at the local tackle shops. Also, from having caught several large trout on these flies.

But wait a minute, I'm confused.
How's that?

A while ago you mentioned a fly called an Adams. Now you say an Adams parachute. Is there a difference?
Good memory. Yes. A parachute is a version of a fly with a single upright ring. It's tied somewhat differently, and it tends to land more gently.

Okay, but why not just ask the guys at the tackle shops and leave it at that?
Because sometimes you can't find the guys at the tackle shops. And sometimes they're wrong. Nobody's perfect, even fly fishers. Besides, it's kind of fun to figure out these things yourself.

That makes sense. But how many of these basic fly types are there?
Four. Or five if you count terrestrials.

Terrestrials?
Land-based insects. Like ants and grasshoppers.

Grasshoppers swim?
No, but they often fall or are blown into the water.

Okay, what are the four types?

Mayflies, caddis flies, midges, and stoneflies. But before getting into the differences among them, it's best to understand what's similar about them.

What's that?

They all live short lives, most of which are spent underwater.

Underwater? Insects don't live under water. They live in the air.

Adult insects live in the air. But nothing starts as an adult, not even us.

You mean insects live underwater as adolescents? Do you suppose we could do that with ours?

As we've said before, we'll do the jokes here. But you're not entirely incorrect. Insects live underwater as eggs, larva, pupae, and nymphs.

Nymphs? Sounds interesting.

Ah! You've read *Lolita*. But she was a nymphette. That's another pursuit altogether.

Back to the insects. How do they get into the water? And how do they get out?

The eggs get into the water because that's where the female deposits them after she mates. Some females just drop the eggs on the surface; others dive down to the bottom of the lake or stream. By and by, the eggs hatch. Then the little hatchlings (the different species go under different names at this stage) struggle to the surface (though some species live underwater for quite a while), and those who survive try to make their way into the air, for one purpose and one alone.

Which is?

Love.

Love?

Well, mating. We're not really sure about the intensity of the relationships, the interinsectial communication, if you will.

I won't. So they mate. Then what?

They die.

Just like that?

Pretty much. It's a short and happy life, at least for the ones who survive to mate. The female, as we said, deposits her eggs first in some way. Then she dies. The fellas just drop dead.

I hope we're not regarding this as a metaphor for the human condition.

Not a bit. For one thing, insects can't fly fish.

Well, if they spend their adulthood in the air, when do the fish eat them?

In just about every other stage, which is a big majority of their lives. Many of them are adults for only a day or a few hours. The fancy name for mayflies—Ephemeroptera—describes how fleeting their lives are. Caddises live longer, sometimes for a few weeks, but from our perspective, even they die young.

Quel dommage. Do fish eat the eggs?

No, but they eat the larvae as they swim to the surface, the sitting (or, in some cases, molting) new adults on the surface or in the surface film, and the spent bodies that drop on the surface after mating.

And do we have flies that imitate all those stages?

Yup. The larvae struggling to the surface are imitated by nymphs and wet flies.

Ah, nymphs again. We haven't really dealt with those yet.

No, we haven't. But we will. In fact, we'll devote most of an entire chapter to nymph and wet fly fishing. It's a slightly different technique from dry fly fishing, and it can be very, very productive.

Is this getting complicated?

No, we're just introducing a little variety. When we get there you'll see how simple it really is.

I hope so. So what are the differences among mayflies, caddises, and the others?

For operational purposes, the differences are not that important, except that stoneflies are bigger, and midges, as you might imagine, are smaller. The basic scientific difference is that midges and caddises have a complete metamorphosis.

Metamorphosis! This is beginning to sound like biology class.

Oh, relax. Actually, we never metamorphosis we didn't like. It just means they go through both a larva and a pupa stage between egg and adulthood. Mayflies and stoneflies skip the pupa stage, though some mayflies do molt several times as they sit on the water.

What does all this mean to me, the beginning fly fisher?

You'll be delighted to know we'll now start simplifying.

Indeed I am.

For dry fly fishing, forget about stoneflies, unless you want to hit the salmon fly hatch on the Madison River in Montana in late June. And right now, you're not ready for trout that big. Stonefly nymphs are another matter, but we'll deal with them in the nymphing chapter.

Good. We're down to three kinds.

No, really two kinds of water insects, because unless you're going to fish in the winter, we'll forget about midges, too. For our purposes we'll stick to mayflies, caddises, and terrestrials.

Tell me more about terrestrials.

A very important question. In the middle of the summer, in the middle of the day, when nothing is hatching and the fish are staying down deep, one of the best ways to bring them up, in some places, are with imitation ants, beetles, or (especially) grasshoppers.

In which places, and why especially grasshoppers?

In places where the stream runs through meadows or open fields, from which land-based insects fall into the water. And especially hoppers because they're nice and easy to see and because when a nice fish takes one it fairly explodes out of the water at it. It's one of the fly fishing's great joys, even if you don't land the fish.

Actually, this has been very interesting. But when I get down to the stream and see a bunch of flies swarming, how on earth am I going to know whether they're mayflies or caddis flies?

You aren't. And you don't have to know. As we've said, if you can get some information from the locals, you're in better shape. But if you can't, and you haven't been informed ahead of time that a certain kind of hatch is likely at the time of year and the time of day you're fishing, you can still examine the flies (catch a few; it's easy) and figure out the three basics.

Which are?

Size, color, and shape.

Right. Even I can do that. It's simple.

Well, we'll make it a little more complicated. Size really means length. Shape refers for the most part to the wings and tails. If the naturals you catch in your hat (some folks take a little fly net with them, but a hat is just as good) have slender tails and tent-shaped wings held upright like little sails, they're almost certainly mayflies, but all you have to know is that the artificial you tie onto your tippet should have tails and tent-shaped wings that look like miniature sails. If the naturals have wings folded along their bodies, they're probably caddises. Look in your fly box for an artificial that looks the same.

That doesn't sound too hard. What about color?

Nine times out of ten, the flies you catch will be a dull color—gray or a muddy brown—which helps camouflage them against the streambed. But some are a lighter gray, almost to the point of being white. One of the best flies for brook trout in the East, especially just before dark, is called a white miller.

Entomology in Your Hat

So I really don't have to know what the flies in the air are called?
I just have to figure out their size, shape, and color?

Right. But here's one warning: The error you're most likely
to make is to use a fly that's too big. When in doubt, go with
a smaller one.

Okay, then I choose my little fly, tie it on, and just do what I did
when I caught my fish the other day?

Well, it also helps if you know where the fish are likely to
be.

How do I find that out?

Read the next chapter.

8.

A READING LESSON OR WHERE THE FISH ARE

All right, here's the first question: What are we doing at this particular stream, with a camera and without a fly rod?

That's three questions, which we'll answer in reverse order. We have no fly rod because a fly rod is like a basketball.

You'll have to explain that.

Just as most of us find it hard to see a basketball sitting there minding its own business without picking it up, twirling it around our back, dribbling it a few times, and launching a shot basketward, even if there's no basket around, so fly fishers find it next to impossible to be at the water with a fly rod without taking just a few casts to see what happens.

And what's wrong with that?

It will detract from our main mission of the day. Which is not to fish this water, but to read it.

Read it? Like a book?

Sort of like a picture book.

And that explains the camera?

Yes. We'll take some pictures so you can look at them later. Also, it's a good idea to bring a camera along anyway, especially if you're planning on releasing most of the fish you catch.

Oh, yeah. Sort of a record of accomplishments.

That, and also so some of your more cynical friends will believe that you actually caught some fish.

Good thought. But what if they think I bought the fish at the store, brought it to the water, and took its picture?

Then your friends are very cynical indeed.

True, but while we're on the subject, what kind of camera should I bring when I fish?

Not a really fine and expensive one. And, for exactly the same reason, not a chintzy one, either.

And what is that reason?

At some point you're going to fall in the water.

I am?

You are. It's nothing to worry about, though, of course, it's better to avoid it. But one of the things a soaking can do is ruin a camera that is either the ultraexpensive kind or its opposite.

Is there a happy medium?

Fortunately, there are cameras that are made to be water-resistant. We're not talking about underwater cameras; they can be quite costly. But there are plenty of water-resistant—

often called "weatherproof"—cameras in a medium price range.

That's good. Now why are we at this particular spot on this stream?

Because this is where the stream bends through the meadow, just a short walk from a little pond. In this way we can, in one stop, learn to "read" both moving water and still water.

Hey, you think of everything, don't you? So we learn to read on this trip, and after that we just fish?

No. Even when you bring your rod and intend to use it, it's a good idea to read water, or at least scan it for a while before starting to fish. It's tempting just to wade out and start casting. But it isn't very smart. If you take time first to look around, your chances of catching fish are much better.

I see. Last chapter we learned about insects; this chapter we learn about water. Do we have to learn words like hydrology?

Nope. Actually, we're not going to learn about water as

such. We're going to learn about fish in water. About where they're likely to be.

Great. Where can they be?

Oh, they *can* be anywhere. And you can catch them anywhere. But they're more *likely* to be in certain places, and if you know where those places are, you're far more likely to catch them.

Okay. Where are they?

Well, let's ask you a question: If you were a fish, where would you be?

Listen! Is this going to be like one of those games that asks me what color I'd be if I were a color or what kind of animal I'd be if I were an animal?

Not at all, not at all. Though we certainly know what we'd be if we were an animal.

What?

A moose.

A moose? Why?

Because then we'd always have a place to hang our hat. But enough of this persiflage. We asked where you'd be if you were a fish because if the predator understands his prey, he or she can find it better.

Makes sense. Let's see. Where would I be if I were a fish?I know. Somewhere warm, right?

Well, that depends on what kind of fish you are. If you're a bass, you'd want fairly warm water. But trout prefer cooler water. They don't just prefer it; they need it. When the water temperature gets above 75 degrees, trout die.

Then how do they live in southern rivers?

Mostly, they don't. Where they're stocked, they rarely live through the summer, so those rivers have to be stocked again. But let's forget temperature for now. We're not at all like fish, temperaturewise; they're cold-blooded. But there's one thing both fish and people need.

Food?

Correct. And fish, being little things with a different metabolism, need it more often, at least during the times of year we're likely to be fishing for them. So, still trying to take the fish's perspective, if you were a fish, where would you go to get food?

Into the current?

Why?

Because food is carried by the current. The little dead bug bodies on the water or the larvae underneath the surface are borne along by the current. A fish could just stay in one place and let the food come to him, instead of wandering all over the place.

Good, except for one little thing.

What's that?

It takes a lot of energy just to *stay* in the current. A fish holding in a strong current might find a lot of food passing by, but he'd burn as much energy just staying where he is as he would gain by eating all that food.

Oh. Good point. Well, then, I guess if I were a fish, I wouldn't stay *in* the current, but *near* it, sort of at its edge.

Quack!

Quack? Why quack?

Because you have said the secret word. And back when America was a great nation and "You Bet Your Life" was

TV's biggest game show, if someone said the secret word a toy duck dropped down from the ceiling and said "quack" and Groucho Marx awarded the person a hundred dollars. You don't win a hundred dollars.

What did I say? Near?

No. Edge. Just remember this magic sentence: Fish live on the edge.

You mean like movie stars, divorce lawyers, and levereged buyouters?

Not exactly. Fish are much smarter, or at least saner. But the basic point to remember is that fish live—and, more important to our task—fish *eat* almost anyplace in a stream or pond where something borders on something.

You mean along the bank?

We mean along either bank, near weeds, behind or in front of rocks, boulders, bridge supports, old tires, fallen tree trunks, big logs, an abandoned '57 Chevy, or anything else that breaks the normal flow of the current. And this also means wherever there are natural changes in the current.

What do you mean by that?

In a few minutes we'll give you brief definitions of the terms fly fishers use for this: pocket water, riffles, pools, and runs. But just remember that anyplace the current stops, or starts, speeds up, slows down, or turns around a bend is a good place to fish. Then you won't have to rememeber the definitions. In fact, one of the best places to fish is right in the middle of the stream, where the current meets the stiller water.

You mean like over there, where the stream widens out and the current slows and the water is deeper for a while?

No. That's a pool, and a pool is your classic great place for fishing. But what we mean is right over there, upstream from the pool, where the water is still flowing fairly fast, but only in the center of the stream. Take a look. For the first six feet or so along the bank, the water is quite still.

Oh, yeah. There's a kind of a seam where the faster water abuts the slow.
Quack again.

Another secret word?
Right. The seam. Fish, especially trout, are likely to hold in the still water right near the current. The current's borderline, so to speak, is called a seam.

I get it. That way the fish can see the food coming down the current, but they can sit where they use less energy.
You got it.

So I guess the first thing to look for when I approach a stream is any of these edge places.
No. Actually, that's the second thing you look for.

What's the first thing?
Fish.

Fish? You can see the fish?
Well, it's not always easy, though those polarized sunglasses we have make it possible. Trout are very well camouflaged, and it's hard to see them in deep water. Sometimes in shallower water you can see their shadows. But the first thing you look for is rise forms.

Rise forms?
Yes. Signs that fish are rising to the surface to eat. Little splashes, the flash of a fin, the concentric circles you also see after you drop a pebble in the water.

That figures. But if I don't see that, then I look for the edges?
Exactly. And you fish there.

Okay. Now can we talk about that pool over there? Just where in the pool are the fish likely to be holding?
Anyplace where there's an edge. That means where the current slows to start the pool (the jargon for this is the head of the pool) or just before it speeds up again at the end (which, you will not be surprised to learn, is called the tail of the pool). Also wherever there's a boulder or fallen log or any other obstruction. And it doesn't have to be an obstruction that sticks above the surface. Look for rock piles or boulders that are entirely underwater, too. And fish along the banks, especially if they're undercut.

Undercut? Are you talking about levereged buyouts again?
Not at all. As the water flows past the bank, it eats it away, leaving a sort of eavelike effect above the waterline. Fish love those little nests because they provide shelter from ospreys, herons, and other birds who love trout even more than we do. And the fish especially like those spots if they are overhung by leafy branches from which little morsels can drop on the water.

Okay. Now what about a little farther upstream, where a small brook enters the larger stream?
Another great place to fish. Where those currents come together there could be a veritable smorgasbord of insect life, just perfect for the fish.

Fine. Are we ready for the definitions?
Yes, although they're kind of vague. A pool is easy to see. A pool is a pool is a pool.

I thought you didn't like Gertrude Stein.
We don't, but sometimes these paraphrases are appropriate.

True. What's between the pools?

The faster water between pools is called a riffle if it's very shallow and kind of wide, and a run if it's a little deeper and narrower.

So what's the pocket water?

It's a riffle or a run with lots of rocks and boulders.

Does any of that make any difference?

Not so's you can tell.

Is that about it?

That's about enough for our purposes in the stream. Now let's climb out and walk over to that little pond to learn how to read still waters.

Which run deep.

Deeper, anyway.

Uh-oh. Now that we're here, I an see that everything I just learned is useless. This looks like just one big, undifferentiated blob of water. I need an entirely new lesson.

No seven-syllable words, please. And no, you don't. We're still looking for edges, though we admit they're a little harder to find in a pond or a lake than in a stream.

Where are they?

First of all, even a lake has banks.

So it does.

And along those banks, the water tends to be shallower, which is what we want.

We do? Aren't the fish often deep?

Often. but for us fly fishers, they're pretty much out of reach. The deepest you can get with a fly is about 30 feet, and that's when you're past the beginner stage. At any rate, fish in lakes and ponds tend to do much of their feeding in the shallower water.

That's good to know. But where are the other edges?

Inlets and outlets, just as in streams. There are also weedbeds, rock piles, and points. The pointier those points are, the better the fishing, especially if, as in the streams, there are overhanging branches above them.

Now that you mention it, I do see some gunky weeds in the water over there.

Yes, and there are other gunky weed patches you don't see because they're totally submerged. So you really have to look for them. And there's another thing to look for.

What's that?

Drop-offs. The bottoms of lakes and ponds are not parking lots. There are deeper spots and shallower spots. The line where the bottom drops down is a seam no less than the current line in a river. Fish hang around those spots.

Well, you're right again. On further review, as they say in the NFL, this pond isn't so undifferentiated. But one thing I've learned today bothers me.

What's that?

So many of these great fishing places—along the weedbeds in the pond here, or under the overhanging branches near the banks of the stream—those are places where it will be hard to cast without getting my fly caught in the leaves, or along the bank. How do I avoid that?

Tant pis, you can't entirely. That is one of the many little complications of our entire enterprise. Opportunity means risk. To succeed, one must dare to fail.

I was afraid you'd say that. Well, maybe for now I'll just fish in the middle of the pools, or along those seams where the current meets the slower water. There are no complications there.

That's what you think.

9.

BASIC DRY
FLY TACTICS
OR
LIFE CAN BE A DRAG

Now, this is more like it. I prefer coming to the water with my fly rod than with just the camera.

Good. But did you bring the camera, too?

Yup. Got it right down here in this big vest pocket.

Well, you ought to move it. That pocket's too low, and the camera is likely to get wet.

Oh. Where should I put it?

In that higher pocket on the left, the one that's sort of where the breast pocket of your suit jacket would be. And it wouldn't be a bad idea to loop the camera strap around your neck, too.

Once again you make sense. Now here we are at that same pool we saw on our reading lesson. I'm going to read it. What do I look for first?

Fish. Or signs thereof.

Hmm. I don't see any.

No. It's too hot and quiet now for there to be much action in the pool. Let's start off by fishing this slightly faster-flowing riffle just upstream from the pool. It has slower water along the banks and current in the middle, a very typical situation. Once again, look for signs of fish.

Oh, right. Rise forms. Why, by gum! There are some right there, near the far bank. Let's go get 'em.

Let's first figure out *how* we're gonna go get 'em. Otherwise we might go spook 'em.

Spook 'em?

Scare them away. Fish can see. And while they can't hear very well, they can sense noise and vibrations in the water. If they know you're around, they won't be.

That's hardly sporting of them.

They're not the ones who have to be sporting. We are.

Okay. How do I not spook them?

First, you should know that trout, and most other fish in creeks and rivers, face upstream.

Always?

No, they swim around some. But their default position, as the computer boys would say, is to look upstream, whence cometh their food. So if you're going to fish upstream—meaning if that's the direction in which you'll be casting—you'll want to approach from downstream.

Wouldn't it be best to get as close as possible along the bank, even before entering the water?

Not always. You'll make less noise that way, but you also might cast a bigger shadow. So sometimes—for instance, if there are no trees along the bank and it's a sunny day—you're better off wading. If you must approach over land, stay low.

Anything else?

Yes. If possible, keep the sun behind you. Unlike us, the fish are not wearing polarized sunglasses, and since they can't even squint, it's harder for them to see into the sun. Also, if there's wind, try to keep that behind you, too, because in general it's easier to cast in the wind's direction than into it.

What if the sun and the wind aren't coming from the same direction?

So far, no one has figured out how to convince either one of them to change. That's usually left to a higher authority. Just go with the flow. If it's a big wind, it becomes more important. If it's just a breeze, I'd try to keep the sun behind me.

All right. But in this case, there's not much wind, the sun is behind me, and the fish I see are all the way across the stream. It's okay to wade on this side of the bank, isn't it?

Yes, because we're not right at the pool, where the water's very quiet. Some of this is just common sense. The stiller the water, the quieter you have to be and the softer you have to wade. In faster water, you don't have to be quite as careful. So let's go to that riffle, the faster stretch beyond the pool, and approach the fish from behind them.

Fine. Now you said one thing I have to decide is whether I'm going to cast upstream or down. Which do I want?

In dry fly fishing, you'll usually want to cast upstream from the fish and let the fly drift down over him. There are exceptions, but we won't get into them.

Well, here I am, and they're still feeding over there, in the slowish water near the far bank. I'm in the slow water near this bank. Those rise forms are about 30 feet straight across from me, and the current is between me and the fish.

You've got the situation right. Now deal with it.

Okay. I'm just going to cast straight across the stream, land my fly a few feet upstream from those fish, and hope its the right kind of fly. If it is, one of them should take it, right?

Maybe.

You're such a grouch. Okay, I'm feeding out line, I'm doing a few false casts, here's my cast. There. My fly landed just about 5 or 7 feet upstream from the rise forms, and it's heading right toward them. Now it's drifting over them. Nothing.

Try again.

I am. Well, the same thing happened again. Nothing. You don't think I spooked them, do you?

No. That's not the problem.

What then? Is it the wrong kind of fly?

No, probably not. This time, after you cast, look at what happens to the line lying between you and the fly, the part of the line that's in the current. Then look at the fly.

All right. Here I go again. Wait. I see. The current is moving my line fast, so that the line is bending downstream.

Right. And what is that doing to your fly?

It's pulling it along at the speed of the current. It's almost got a wake behind it.

No almost about it.

Well, is that good? It gets the fly over more fish in less time.

No, it is not good. Fish eat insects. They do not eat out-board motorboats. Even though we're using an attracter fly again, one that isn't designed to imitate a particular insect, it does have to resemble insectitude in general. Even a fish is smart enough not to try to eat something moving that fast.

Oh. Is this a common problem?

Very. It is known as drag.

Oh, no. I'm fishing in drag?

No, you're fishing *with* drag. Which means you're really not fishing at all. When your fly is zipping through the water like that, you might as well be playing mah-jong for all the fish you'll catch.

If I don't want drag, what do I want?

What you want is a natural drift when the fly flows over the fish, or the place where you think fish are. In a stream, eventually every cast will end in drag. The trick is to avoid drag during the most productive parts of the fly's downstream journey.

And how do I get this natural drift?

There are a few ways. Right now you've got three options.

And Option One is?

Move.

Move?

Right. Instead of casting to those rise forms from across the stream, wade downstream and then go across to the side where the fish are. Then you can cast straight upstream to them.

You mean, just try to put the fly right on top of the fish?

No, you still want the fly to land a few feet upstream from him. But since your line won't be in the current, you won't get drag until the fly has gone way past the fish. Probably not until it's gone past you.

But won't I get slack in the line as soon as the fly starts heading back toward me?

You will if you don't start stripping in as soon as the fly hits the water.

I see. But here's another question: Won't the fish be spooked by my fly line zipping over his head?

Maybe. That's one reason why Option One isn't so good. Of course, if your cast is very, very accurate and your presentation is very, very gentle, you can make sure that only the fly and the leader actually land where the fish is. But that's a bit tricky.

A bit too tricky for me right now, I fear. What's Option Two?
Raise your rod.

Explain
If you stay where you are and cast just as you did before, but raise your rod by its butt as high over your head as possible, you'll delay the onset of drag, perhaps long enough for your fly to get a natural float over the fish.

But then won't I have a lot of trouble setting the hook?
Yes. That's the problem with Option Two.

Great. Lets hear Option Three.
Promise you won't hate us?

I already hate you. Let's hear it.
Put slack in your line.

Put slack in my line. Now I've heard everything .A couple of chapters ago you kept bugging me to keep my rod tip up so I wouldn't have any slack in my line. Now you want me to put slack in my line? Is this not a violation of a basic precept?
Yes. What do you think basic precepts are for? As you cast, check your rod at about the ten o'clock position, pull the butt of the rod back toward you just a touch, and quickly drop that butt to waist level.

Drop the butt?
And boogie. No. Don't boogie. Just try one cast that way.

It sounds complicated. I'm not sure I can remember all that.
Well, actually, you don't have to. The important thing is just to interrupt your forward cast, somewhat jerkily, and then

maybe shake your butt from side to side a little bit as the line is stretching out over the water.

Shake my butt from side to side? This does sound like dancing lessons. Okay. Here I go, unlearning what I so carefully learned before. Stop the forward cast, pull the butt, drop the butt. Hey, look at that! There are little wrinkles in the line.

Right. And they have to straighten out before drag begins.

Well, you've solved one problem, but I've still got another. It's not as bad as holding my rod up to the heavens, but this doesn't make setting the hook any easier, either.

True enough. Like life, fly fishing is a series of trade-offs. Ideally, you can time the cast so the slack is just about out of the line, but drag has not set in just as the fly is floating over the fish.

And unideally? Which seems to be the norm?

You can help idealness by stripping in, getting the slack out of the line just as you see the fly heading over the fish.

And failing that?

You just have to set the hook a bit harder. Lock the line against the rod with the index finger of that rod hand, and as soon as you see anything at all near where your fly should be, raise that rod tip a bit more than you would if you had no slack.

You mean like *that*. Hey, I got another one.

Yes, you did.

Okay. I don't hate you after all.

Keep that rod tip up.

10.

BASIC OTHER-THAN-DRY-FLY TACTICS

What is this funny-looking thing you have told me to tie onto my tippet?

That's a nymph.

Oh, yeah. A nymph. What is it?

Well, it's a few things, but for now let's just call it one of the sinking flies.

How many kinds of sinking flies are there?

For our purposes, three. Nymphs, streamers, and wet flies.

How do they differ?

In several ways, all of which have exceptions, so let's not bother with most of them. Suffice it to say that streamers are longer and skinnier, and the fish think they are minnows or other small fish, or maybe crayfish.

They do? How do we know?

Well, okay, we don't know. We *think* the fish think they are small fish. But maybe they just strike at them out of anger or curiosity, sort of the way your cat pounces at a string or a feather passing by. And at this point we should tell you that some streamers are called bucktails.

What's the difference between a bucktail and a regular streamer?

They're made differently, but let's not worry about it.

Okay. Back to the basic three, then. In addition to streamers being longer and skinnier, are there other differences I ought to know?

Sure. Just as a historical point, you might want to know that wet flies were the original flies. When old Izaak Walton, the man who couldn't spell "complete," first waxed philosophical about the art of angling, those were wet flies he and his disputants were using.

Really? Why weren't dry flies used?

Because no one had made metal light enough to float, even with feathers stuck to it.

How do I tell a dry fly from a sinking fly?

Dries are fluffy. Their wings go up, or they have tails or other fluff to keep them afloat. On sinking flies, the wings are swept back, if there are wings.

If streamers may imitate small fish, what do wet flies and nymphs imitate?

Nymphs probably imitate nymphs, or at any rate one of the preadult stages of the various insects as they swim along the bottom or struggle toward the surface. Wet flies also imitate emerging aquatic insects, usually at the stage where they are just below the surface.

The Streamer

The Dry Fly

The Nymph

The Muddler Minnow

Sounds as though there isn't really that much different between them.

There really isn't that much difference among them, to be quite grammatical. But at this point we'll tell you about one very special sinking fly.

Which is?

The muddler minnow. Technically it's a streamer, but it's a streamer specifically designed to imitate a sculpin, a little fish that swims along the bottom. And a muddler minnow may be the single most productive fly in the world.

Okay, but how do I know when to use a dry and when to use a sinking fly?

If nothing at all is rising, you might want to start with sinking flies. Or you could try a dry for a while to see if you can convince something to rise, and if that fails, switch to a wet or a nymph. When the weather is poor, especially if it's chilly, wets or streamers are likely to be more productive than dries.

Well, then, if I decide I do want to use a sinking fly, how do I know which kind to use?

Aside from the tried-and-true scientific method of asking at the local tackle shop, you may not know for sure. But here's another thing you can do: Turn over a few rocks in the stream or along the lake shore, or grab a handful of weeds, see what's under the rocks or on the leaves, and then apply the old tripartite test.

Tripartite test? Ah! I remember. Size, shape, and color.

Bingo. In general, places with big rocks will have larger nymphs, crustaceans, and other underwater life. If all the stone is pebbly, the subsurface fauna will be smaller.

Fauna? I thought we weren't going to get technical.

Sorry.

Are there other rules?

The faster or more discolored the water, the bigger the wet fly you'll want. Try a 10 or even an 8. If the water is clear and not running fast, use a 14 or smaller.

Any other tips?

Yes. Use that other famous scientific technique: trial and error. Try a big brown thing. If that doesn't work after a few minutes, take it off and try a little black thing. If nothing else works, cast a muddler minnow straight across the current and start yanking it back with abrupt, harsh little strips of the line.

It sounds a bit less scientific than dry fly fishing.

It is. But it can be very productive because fish are always feeding under the surface, and they're only occasionally feeding on the surface. Some fly fishers, in fact, use nothing but sinking flies.

Okay, I guess I'm ready to start. I have this nymph tied on. So I guess I cast it just as I would a dry fly, right?

You can try that.

Why don't I like your tone of voice? Well, here I go. I play out some line, I start the backcast of my first false cast, and I . . . *hey!*

Say hey, Willie.

What's *on* that line? It almost took my *ear* off. And it feels *heavy.*

That's because it *is* heavy. These things have to sink. That means we have to put some weight on the line.

Where?

Two places, in this case. The nymph itself is weighted. And as we guess you didn't notice, we put a tiny bit of split shot on the leader about 18 inches above the fly.

Split shot? Oh. I see. This little gray pebble.

Right.

How did you get it? And how did you get it on?

We bought it. And as you can see from this other one here,

it has, as the name implies, a bit of a split, a crevice on one side. You just slip it over the leader and bite it down tight.

Bite? As in, with teeth?

Your dentist would no doubt object, and you can use any one of a number of little tools to do it. But almost everyone just bites. You don't have to bite that hard, and the shot is made of pretty soft lead.

How do I know how much weight to use?

You don't, at first. First of all, it depends how deep you want to get. With most plain wet flies you want to be just below the surface, so you don't need much weight. Maybe you don't need any, just some sinking gunk on the fly. For nymphs and streamers you want to get deeper. You want your fly to tick the bottom now and again, but not get hung up there. And the faster the water, the more weight you'll need to get to the depths you want.

So I do trial and error again? Adding or subtracting weight until I get it right?

Afraid so. Although if you're not getting quite deep enough, you can first try just yanking the fly back toward you a bit faster. That should make it go a bit deeper.

But how do you cast with this weight?

Shorter, with more difficulty and less finesse. But finesse isn't as necessary with sinking flies. You don't need delicate presentation.

How do I keep it away from my ear?

Do a kind of three-quarter cast, or even sidearm, like a second baseman. You almost want to loft the fly into the air. Also, you really don't have to false cast at all. You're not trying to dry this fly.

Any other differences between this and dry fly fishing?

Several. In the old days, the rule was to fish sinking flies downstream, or straight across. This can still be productive. But most of us now think you're better off casting upstream, letting the fly drift down, and then stripping it back upstream toward you with little strips. You cover more water that way.

Do I not have to worry about drag?

Less, because the naturals are often struggling in the water, going this way and that. Still, the longer your natural-looking, drag-free drift, the more likely you are to get a fish.

All right. I'm going to cast again. Short and sidearm this time. It sure did hit the water with a plunk.

Don't worry about that.

Hey! I think I got something.

You do. You have a rock on the bottom.

How do you know?

Because there's no action on your line. Fish, as you have already seen, thrash around when caught. Rocks do not.

Now what do I do?

The same thing you do when you catch a tree on the bank. Wade over there and pull it out.

What if this were farther away, or across deeper water, and I couldn't get there?

Then point your rod tip right at the fly, and pull on *the line* only, not the rod. Your fly should pop loose.

And if it doesn't?

Then your tippet will snap, and you tie on another fly.

Catching Rocks with
Weighted Flies

Okay, I have it. Now, does catching the rock mean I was too deep?

Probably. Take the split shot off. Maybe the weight on the nymph itself was enough in this case.

All right. Here I go again. Yes, this is better. I can feel that the fly is zipping along near the bottom, but not on it. But wait.

Wait for what?

Why did my line just sort of hang in place for a minute instead of following the fly downstream?

Probably because you had a fish.

I did? I didn't feel a thing.

You often don't when fishing sinking flies. If there's any

slack in the line at all, you probably won't feel a thing. The best advice is to set the hook if you see anything unusual at all, very definitely including when you see your line stop.

Explain a little more, please.

When you fish any kind of sinking fly, you can only see the line, not the fly. Keep your eye on the line where it goes into the water. Follow that line-water connecting point with your rod tip, stripping in slack as the line gets closer to you. And watch for anything—a twitch or a tightening of the line, any kind of interruption of its downstream voyage.

What about when I'm pulling the fly back upstream?

Good question. In the first place, half the time you'll think you have a fish just because of the tension of the current against the fly. Also, keep your rod at pretty much of a 90-degree angle to the line, because if you do get a strike, the combined force of the fish and the current can snap off the tippet.

How will I know the difference between the current and a fish?

In this case, you probably will feel it. After you've caught one or two while stripping upstream in a current, you'll learn the difference.

Hmmm. Sounds difficult. Isn't there another way to know if you've got a strike?

Yes. You can use a strike indicator, though some purists will exile you to deepest Siberia.

What's a strike indicator?

It's a little, bright-colored bit of yarn or plastic you wrap around your line or around the butt of your leader. If it gets pulled under the surface, you've probably got a fish.

Why do the purists object?

Some liken it to the bobber a worm fisherman uses. But it can be very helpful, especially for a beginner. Or you can use a dropper.

A dropper? What's a dropper?

It's another fly, usually a dry, tied onto a separate length of tippet that you attach to your leader about 36 inches above the fly. The dropper floats on the surface, and when you see it go down, set that hook.

Sounds interesting. Is that legal?

Sure. You can fish with three or four flies. It's the common method in Britain.

Oh, those British. Wait. Suppose the dry fly attracts a fish?

All the better.

But how do I tie the dropper onto the leader?

With either a barrel or a surgeon's knot, which we'll explain presently.

You mean now?

No, we mean presently, which means pretty soon, no matter how often it's misued to mean "now."

This is getting interesting. What else should I know?

In this kind of fishing, you'll often get your strike near the end of your drift, or even on the retrieve as you're stripping back in. So do that with short, little jerks.

Short, little jerks?

Not like the nerd in the office next to you. Just bring in line a few inches at a time. And wiggle your butt a bit. Flip your rod around.

Just like the president?

You, too, can grow up to be one.

11.

OF BASS AND OTHER BREEDS

Why are we back here at the spot where the river bends close to the pond? This isn't another insect lesson, is it?

Not at all. Today, you'll note, we have our rods.

Yes, and I also note we have bigger leaders, 2X and even OX, and funny-looking big flies, even bigger than streamers. What are they for?

Bass.

Bass? I thought bass were the fish caught by those guys who fish in tournaments, guys who throw huge gobs of metal and plastic deep into the water.

They are.

And I thought all that was the antithesis of fly fishing?

It is. It is.

So why are we fishing for bass?

Because bass is the great American fish. It's found everywhere, it puts up a great fight, and catching them on a fly
rod is one of life's joys.

As great a joy as catching a trout?

Well, that's all very subjective. A bass isn't quite as pretty
as a trout. What is? And it doesn't taste as good. But it's a
magnificent game fish.

But I can't get a fly way down there where those tournament
competitors catch bass.

No, you can't. Not that it's impossible with a fly rod, but it's all but impossible at your level of expertise, and explaining how to do that is beyond the scope of this book. Happily, though, bass often feed in shallow water. Especially smallies.

Smallies?

Basically, we fish for two kinds of bass, both of which are black bass, which come in two varieties, smallmouth and largemouth.

What's the difference between them?

You'd think the big difference would be that smallies have smaller mouths. Actually, their mouths aren't so much smaller as lower.

Lower?

Yes. The jaw of a largemouth bass extends above its eye. The smallie's does not. Largemouth bass grow larger, though, of course, a big smallie is bigger than a small largemouth. Largemouths are greenish-black, while smallmouth bass are usually bronze or even brown, which is why they are sometimes called bronzebacks.

If the smallies often feed in shallow waters, where do you catch largies?

Nobody calls them largies.

Okay. Where do you catch largemouth bass?

Well, they sometimes feed in shallow waters, too. But they're far less likely to be found in streams or rivers. They like lakes and ponds. Smallies often live in the same places trout do. Largemouth bass prefer warmer water. But the great thing about them is that their range is all over America. Smallies don't thrive in really hot climes.

Any other differences between them?

Smallies like rocky, pebbly streambeds or gravelly lake floors. Largemouth bass prefer muddy or silty bottoms.

Let's start with the largemouths. What do they eat?

Everything. Little bugs and big rodents.

Big rodents?

Well, pretty big. They love mice, and getting one to ambush your imitation mouse is, shall we say, a memorable experience.

You said they often feed in shallow waters. But do they ever take food from the surface?

Oh, yes. Early in the morning and at dusk they grab things right off the top, and that's the best time to get them.

Where do you find them?

Well, the same place you find any fish. At an edge. But the very best way to catch largemouth bass is right in the middle of some weeds or lilies.

Won't my fly get caught on the weeds?

Yes. Most bass flies come with weedguards, usually just a strip of fairly thick monofilament stretched across the hook. This minimizes, but does not eliminate, getting hung up in vegetation.

Another one of our risk-versus-reward situations?

Exactly.

Okay. What about the smallies? What do they eat?

Everything. They are not picky eaters. You can catch them on small dry flies, on nymphs, and on muddler minnows. But what we're going to use for all bass now are poppers.

Poppers?

So called because when you move them through the water, they go "pop," a pleasing sound to two animals.

Which two?

The fly fisher, just because it's fun to hear. And the bass, because he thinks it's a meal.

Wait. I thought I was supposed to land my dry flies softly and quietly on the surface.

Not your bass bug. In many ways, fly fishing for bass is easier than trout fishing. Casting accuracy can still be important, but you don't have to worry about presentation. In fact, you want to slap that bug on the water. And while sometimes you'll see bass feeding, you're more likely to fish blind.

Blind? You mean where you just hope there's a fish somewhere?

Well, a fish that eats a mouse or even a large bug is not a constant sipper, as trout often are. Bass wait for a good meal to come along, pounce on it, and then go below for a civilized meal, though to the best of our knowledge they do not finish up with coffee and a cigar. But eating a mouse takes a few minutes.

Well, all right. Here we are at the pond, and I see a big glop of lilies over in that little inlet, where the water is shallow and the bottom is muddy. Is that a possible bass hangout?

For largemouth it certainly is. Cast right into the middle of the leaves. As with a weighted line for sinking flies, you don't have to false cast and you'll want to sort of lob your fly over there.

Wait. That didn't come anywhere near where I was aiming.

No. It takes a few minutes to get the hang of it, just as it did with the weighted nymph.

I'll try again. Uh-oh. It landed right on that big leaf.

Maybe your guard worked. Give a bit of pull and see if the fly comes loose.

Nope. Golblast it. It's stuck. Now what do I do?

Don't pull hard. Try wiggling your rod.

That didn't work either.

Okay. Then grab the line just in front of your reel and quickly tighten and release, tighten and release, sort of the same principle you use when you rock a car that's stuck in the snow.

All right. Ah, it worked. My fly's loose.

Good. Try again.

Okay. Now I think I've got it. There. It landed in the water right near a big old leaf. Now what do I do?

Let it sit there.

Sit there? For how long?

For a good minute. One trick is not to move the fly until all the circles in the water it made when it hit have disappeared. And while you're waiting, point the rod tip at the fly. You want to keep your rod tip fairly low. And don't shake your rod. In this kind of fishing you want to move only the line, not the rod.

Well, the circles have disappeared. Now what?

Now we come to the crux of a major philosophical dispute. It pits the school of quick-and-short retrieves against the school of long-and-slow retrieves, and while it probably lacks the profundity of the differences between the Schools of Hillel and Shamai, or even the Roundheads and the Flatheads, plenty of words have been used to present the opposing arguments.

What's your position?

We are ever ecumenical, if only because variety is more fun. Try a tiny little retrieve at first. Pull that popper toward you about an inch.

Only an inch? How can I do that?

It's not easy. Try wrapping the line just once around your finger. You just want the tiniest, quickest little yank on the line.

There. Now what?

Let it sit.

Nothing's happening.

Okay. Try a longer, slower pull.

All right, I'll . . . *wow*! Look at that. It's an explosion.

No, it's a largemouth. Set the hook.

I did. And I thought I did it fast. But I lost him.

Yes, you did.

Why?

Because you set the hook as you would for a trout.

Isn't that the way to do it for a bass?

Not at all. Bass have bigger, tougher mouths.

Why didn't you tell me earlier?

Oh, we thought we'd use failure as a pedagogical technique. Frustration can concentrate the mind quite wonderfully.

Very funny. How do I set the hook for a bass?

Don't lift the rod tip. Keep it low at first. Instead, give the line a firm, steady pull with your line hand. Then do it again, this time lifting the *butt* of the rod, not the tip, just a bit.

Keep the rod tip down. Then continue pulling on the line with short jabs. After a few of them, the hook should be set.

Then do I play it as I would a trout?
Then you play it as you would any fish at all.

Okay, I'm going to wait a minute and then try again.
Good idea. And let's give you a little tip. This time, just before the fly hits the water, grab the line with your line hand and pinch it against the rod.

Why?
You'll have less slack at the moment your fly hits. Sometimes you get your strike right then.

All right, here I go. Backcast, lob it forward, grab and pinch, and it hits the water, and . . . *wow*! Here I go again. Another explosion.
Right again. Keep the rod tip low and pull, firmly but not jerkily, on the line.

I am. I think I have him now.
Okay. Now get your rod tip up, and strip in as you can.

Got it. *Hey!* Look at him jump. He's huge.
And you remembered to bow your rod as he jumped. Good for you. Actually, for a bass he's average. About a foot long, I'd say.

Seems huge to me. Should I bring him in real slowly?
Not too slowly. That big tippet can take a lot more punishment than the smaller ones we use for trout. On the other hand, they're real fighters, so don't just try to horse him to you.

No, I won't. I've got him now, though.
Good job.

But I've got some questions. First, should I have done anything different had that been a smallmouth bass?

No, not really. You find them in different places. You fish them pretty much the same.

Next, do I always use surface flies for bass?

Oh, no. You can catch bass under the surface with nymphs and streamers. When nymphing in rivers for smallies your best bet is to cast up and across, allowing the nymph to drift with the current.

What kind of subsurface flies would I use?

A great bass fly is called a Dahlberg Diver. And one superb way to bass fish is to use it on a dropper, with a surface popper on the main tippet. Fish them near logs, rocks, or drop-offs. Vary the retrieve, even to the point of making it a bit rambunctious.

Suppose I want to get a fly a bit deeper.

Try a size 4 or 6 woolly bugger with a piece of split shot right on its nose.

Will I be able to feel a strike on a subsurface fly?

That could be a problem. You might want to consider a strike indicator if you're not using a dry-fly dropper.

And finally, can I catch other kinds of fish with flies?

You can catch just about anything with flies. In fact, as we said at the start, one of the easiest and most enjoyable kinds of fly fishing is for bluegills.

Actually, what are the differences among a bluegill, a sunfish, a bream, and a crappie?

Well, there are differences, but some of them are just regional names for the same fish, and we can really consider them as one. The true bluegill, though, is bigger, and therefore the most fun.

Where are they?

Where aren't they?

What do you catch them on?

What do you not? Many fly fishers prefer bass bugs, but trout flies will do just fine. Small panfish (for such is the general name for all the above species) are more likely to feed on the surface, but you can catch very nice bluegills on dry flies. For crappie, which feed deeper in ponds and lakes, you'll want to use something that gets deeper.

What about bigger fish, such as walleyes or pike?

Walleyes like minnows. They also like bright colors. Use red or yellow streamers, something like a fairly large Mickey Finn.

How about perch?

They're a bit boring to catch but great to eat. They're in smallish streams in shallow, warm spots, and they often travel in schools. If you get one, you can probably get enough in the same spot to feed the whole family.

12.

JUST A FEW SLIGHTLY ADVANCED TECHNIQUES

Why are we here in the late afternoon, with chest waders instead of hip boots and only a few, very light leaders?

Well, this is a combination of your final exam and your final real lesson.

Already? You mean I have nothing more to learn?

Oh, you have a lot more to learn, and we're going to teach you some if it now. But then, as we told you at the beginning, some of it we're not going to teach you at all. This is a beginner's book, and you have now begun.

Really? How have I done?

So far, very well. Perhaps too well. We didn't want to discourage you, and we wanted to telescope things, so we had you catch those fish. But remember, we're making this up. In real life, many a beginning fly fisher doesn't get a strike his or her first time or two out, and doesn't actually land one during the first season's effort.

That sounds discouraging.

It can be. So we're telling you now that this could happen. And here's something else that can happen.

More bad tidings? What?

Kind of bad. You'll forget some of what you've learned. A lot of it, such as where to find the fish or how to figure out what kind of fly to use, you can remind yourself simply by scanning through the book again. But if you don't practice regularly, your casting skills will probably deteriorate, too.

Oh. I was hoping it was kind of like learning to swim or ride a bike, that once you learn you can't forget.

Not quite. You won't totally forget. But you'll forget part of it and develop a bad habit or two, enough to throw you off and make your line, leader, and fly land in a clump 3 feet in front of you or something like that.

How do I avoid that?

You know how to get to Carnegie Hall?

Sure. Just walk up Seventh Avenue to Fifty-seventh Street.

No. Practice. Practice.

Oh, I get it. Well, as long as we're here, should we proceed with the final lesson and the test? The sun is starting to go down, and there are 12 million little bugs in the air.

Exactly where we begin.

Where?

With the bugs. Catch a few. There'll be plenty left.

Ah. Of course. This is a hatch.

Right. Grab your hat, wave it through a swarm, and see what you've got.

A hat for the hatch. Got some.

Tell us about them.

Well, let's see, this will take some examination because they're quite small. They're light-colored, a sort of creamy brown. There are little, upswept wings near the head and a tiny wisp of a tail.

Good. What does that tell you?

That it's probably a mayfly, but that I definitely want a small, cream-colored fly with wings and a tail. Now, the question is whether I have one.

Look in your fly box.

Here's one. What's this called?

We haven't the foggiest idea.

You don't? I thought you were experts.

We told you we weren't. Actually, the foggiest idea is just about what we have. We think it's something called a Hendrickson.

You think? You don't know?

Don't be alarmed. First of all, as we said before, these names are unofficial. What some people call a Hendrickson, others call a blue dun.

Well, does it look like these natural insects?

Apply the tripartite test.

It's the right color. It's the right shape. Is it too big?

To ask certain questions is to answer them. The answer to "Should we punt?" is always yes. The answer to "Is that Sinatra or one of the other guys?" is always one of the other guys. The answer to "Is this fly too big?" is always yes.

Okay. I've got a smaller version. How small is this?
Looks like a 20. Tie it on.

Fine. Wait a minute. Why can I hardly see the end of this tippet?
Well, you chose a #20 fly. So we gave you a 5X tippet, which is .006 inch in diameter.

Can't I use a bigger one?
Some would say you should use a 6X, which is smaller, but our theory is always to use the thickest possible tippet because the fish is less likely to break it off, making both him and you very unhappy. But if you have trouble turning over the fly with that leader, we may switch to a 6X.

Well, I have to tell you that it is extremely difficult to thread this through this tiny hole in the fading light.
This is probably a good time to bring up the advice to get one of those little magnifying glass doohickies (technically known as a magnifying loupe; obviously it was invented by a guy who couldn't spell "loop") that you screw into the inside of your hat brim. It's very helpful, especially if you're in or approaching those in-between years.

Which in-between years are those?
Not old enough to be impotent but too old for adultery.

Well, I finally got it. Now what?
Read the river.

I really don't have to. Those little bugs have started to fall, and the fish have started to take them off the surface. There are rise forms and rising fish everywhere.
Okay. Pick out a spot.

There seem to be several fish feeding right across the stream near the far bank over there.

Wade in and start casting.

Wait. I can see on this first cast that I'm going to have a real drag problem. There's about 10 feet of fast current between me and the fish in the slower water near the other bank.

The first thing to do is to see if you can stand in that current. But I think it's too deep and too fast.

It is. Now what do I do?

Mend line.

My line's not broken.

Mending line doesn't mean repairing it. It means giving it an upstream flip to put a big belly in the line.

No more anatomical jokes, please. Just explain.

Hold the rod low in front of you. Then, keeping your arm as stiff as possible, roll your wrist toward the upstream direction. That flips the middle of the line upstream. Until that belly straightens out, you'll have a natural drift.

Well, it put a belly in the line, and now I've got a natural drift. But the mend itself made the fly move a few feet at roughly the speed of light.

Yes, it will do that. You can minimize it by releasing some slack line as you make the mend. But since you know where your fish are, just make sure that you get your natural drift starting about 5 feet upstream of them. Mending your line before you get to that point does no harm. And here's another idea.

What's that?

Do a reach cast.

How do I do that?

It's basically just mending line while it's in the air. Just before your line hits the water, move your rod upstream. This puts the belly in the line without zipping the fly along the water.

That's all well and good, but how do I know when to mend, or how hard a reach cast to make, to get my natural drift when I want it?

The old trial-and-error method.

All this stripping in and recasting is tiring, and it might be scaring the fish.

Well, you can try a roll cast.

What's that?

Raise your rod straight up and a bit off to your right (to your left if you're a lefty). Now come to a complete stop for a few seconds. Then, as forcefully as you can with your wrist and forearm, snap the rod tip straight down in front of you. The line should come up and roll back onto the water right in front of you.

Why don't I just do that all the time?

Well, with no backcast or false casting, you can't dry your fly. Also, you can't get as much distance. It's mainly helpful when your line is in the water in one spot and all of a sudden you see a fish somewhere else.

Now I'm having another problem: My leader isn't really straightening out. Is it too heavy? Do I need a 6X?

Maybe. But first let's try something else.

What's that?

Well, we're going to break another rule here.

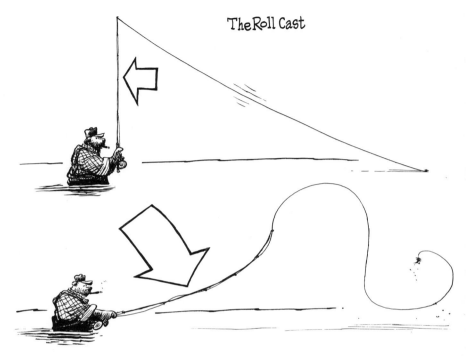

The Roll Cast

Which one this time?

The one that tells you not to follow through all the way. On your next cast, first make sure your backcast straightens all the way out; then, when you power it forward, snap your wrist straight down a bit.

But I thought that was forbidden.

It is, in the books. But you're not casting in books. Basically, all these rules are generalizations that you can violate under certain conditions if the violations help. We've found that this wrist snap, if it's done straight down, can make for a better cast.

All right, I'll try it. A few false casts to get my bearings and dry

the fly. Backcast all the way back, power it forward, snap the wrist. You're right. It worked. But you know what?

What?

The fish are about 5 feet farther away than I'm able to reach.

Well, it's time to shoot line.

And how do I do that?

Pull a few more feet of line off the reel and hold it with your line hand. Don't leave any slack in the part of the line that's between your hand and the rod. Just leave the slack line in the water. Cast as you normally would, holding the line tight in your line band, between your thumb and forefinger. As you're powering forward, shortly before your rod gets back to the vertical, at about the ten-thirty position by the clock, release the line you're holding. It should shoot through the guides and make your cast longer.

What if I cast too far?

That's not too much of a problem. Just strip in or move your rod and skid the fly to the fish.

Well, I'll try it. Hey, that wasn't very hard, and I think I got out there far enough.

Good. Mend the line right about now and you should get the good drift right over the fish.

I do, I do. And I *got one.* I think. Uh, did I lose it?

Well, it took your fly, but you never really had it.

Why?

We think you set the hook too soon.

Too soon? I thought I was supposed to set it as soon as I saw *anything* happening around my fly.

True, but that's another generalization. These are pretty big fish. And remember, you can see him take the fly. One good idea is to wait for his head to go back under the surface. Or count "one, Mississippi." Then, because this is a pretty light tippet, as soon as you set the hook, drop the rod tip for just a second to ease the pressure. Then bring it back up and start stripping line.

All right, I'll try it that way. Again, a few false casts, a complete backcast, power it forward, snap the wrist, mend the line. There he is. Pause for just a second, set the hook, lower the rod tip, bring it back up. *Hey! It's a good one!*

Yes, it is. He's going to want line.

I'm giving it to him. He's heading for those submerged rocks over there. What do I do about that?

Hold the rod high. That should keep him above them.

It worked. Now I'll strip in.

Actually, he's big enough that after you strip in all your slack you might want to play him from the reel.

He's heading upstream.

Go with him. Try not to let him get upstream of you, and try to keep him as close as possible.

There's a jump.

Bow the tip. Good. You've still got him. Now reel in if you can. But if he heads right back downstream toward you, strip in line. You won't be able to reel in fast enough.

I think he's getting tired.

Yes, but he's not done yet.

No, he's not. There's another jump.

Good work. He is pretty tired. Bring him in slowly. I think he'll try another run, but just stay with him.

My goodness, I'm out of breath. Is that physical or psychological?
Yes.

I think I'm getting him.
He's pretty close to you now, but don't overdo it. He still has some energy left, and he could break off that tippet.

Now he's swimming in circles. Should I get my net?
You could. Or you could just bring him to you, reach down the leader to the fly in his mouth, and see if you can twist it out without bothering with the net.

What's the advantage of that?
It's probably better for the fish. You won't be able to take his picture. But you've played this guy for a while, and being out of the water for even a minute or two might not be good for him.

Okay. Here he comes. My, he's big. He's at least 15 inches. Is that a good fish?
It's a lovely fish. It's a rainbow. See that pink stripe along his side?

Yes. What a sleek and pretty animal. Here we go. He's right near me now. I'll reach down and . . . yes, I've got the fly out. It was just inside his jaw. I'm amazed he didn't throw it.
He tried.

He's just sort of sitting here, treading water. No, now he's flipping away. Goodbye, fish. You were great fun.
Great fun?

You know, it was more than that. There was something about it, the combination of exhilaration, anxiety, and satisfaction that was

Releasing the Fish

kind of, well . . . I hesitate to say this, but it's just a touch compara-
ble to another activity I could mention. Has anyone else ever
thought of that?

Only the happy few who've caught a nice rainbow.

13.

WHERE TO GO OR THESE ARE A FEW OF OUR FAVORITE HAUNTS

That was a nice final lesson here at our imaginary river. But now I have to return to real life, which is in a real metropolitan area, and all I know about our local rivers and lakes is that I'm advised neither to drink the water nor to eat the fish in them.

There is a lot of that going around. It's one of the things we who fish should try to do something about. The more clean water, the more fishing. But in the meanwhile, do not despair. There's plenty of fishable water not that far away.

Like where?

You'd be amazed, even if you live smack-dab in the middle of Manhattan, Chicago, or Dallas, how close you are to some

135

Our Favorite Trout Stream

good, old-fashioned farm ponds, many of them just brimming with brim and other good panfish.

But will farmers let you fish in them?
Usually.

For free?
Depends. On both the farmer and you. People usually respond to politeness with politeness. One of the best ways to avoid having to pay is to offer to do so at the outset. But even when a fee is asked for, it's rarely very big.

Okay, but suppose I want to fish in a larger pond or lake, or in a river, and then suppose I live in the middle of New York. Then what do I do?
Actually, some of the most famous trout streams in the

world are in the Catskills. The Beaverkill is always crowded on opening day (that's April 1 in New York; usually too cold). In a sense, the Catskill region is the home of American fly fishing.

Great. I'll head right up there.
Not so fast.

What's the matter?
Not that we want to be discouraging, but those places may be a bit out of your league right now.

How so?
As you'd expect for such good fishing so close to so many people, they're awfully crowded. And the fish are extremely wary. Most of them have been caught before.

What's my next closest alternative?
Pennsylvania. Again, these are famous trout streams. The Letort, the Yellow Breeches, and several other streams just a bit southwest of Harrisburg are teeming with trout.

Okay, I'm off.
Slow down again.

Same reasons?
Yes, plus one more: These are spring-fed creeks. The water is crystal clear. That means you can see the trout.

Isn't that good?
Yes. But they can also see you. And they tend to ignore you.

Well, you've been pretty clever about telling me where *not* to go. How about telling me a good place.
Fair enough. In the Northeast, one of the best fly fishing

rivers, for trout and other species, is the Connecticut. Way up, where it begins below the Connecticut Lakes in New Hampshire, the river is wild and cold and full of trout. Fish the stretch just below Lake Francis with smallish March browns, blue-winged olives, and pale morning duns.

If that's too long a drive for you, just go up to the area around West Cornwall, Connecticut, a place of magical charm. The Housatonic River there is wide and wadable, and while you'll find other fly fishers, it's not nearly as crowded as the Catskills.

That's better. What about when I go down to our nation's capital?

Well, if you really have to, go ahead. And as is true with everything in Washington, there is bad news and good news.

What's the bad news?

Even though you're not all that far south, it's getting a little warm for trout.

What's the good news?

There's some great fly fishing for bass only an hour from the Capitol dome, on the very river that flows nearby.

On the Potomac?

On the Potomac. Just go up to near Harpers Ferry, West Virginia, where old John Brown made all that trouble. The river is wide, but wadable from the banks, especially in mid-summer. In late July, use a #12 white miller. Another good place to go for smallies in the Washington area is the Rappahannock River in Virginia.

But there's no trout around Washington?

Some. There's Mossy Creek, near Harrison, Virginia. That's tough fishing, though, rather like Pennsylvania spring creeks.

Very interesting. Now, suppose I want to hook (you should pardon the expression) my brother-in-law in Chicago on fly fishing. Where should I take him when I go visiting?

To Wisconsin.

Where in Wisconsin?

In general, anyplace in Wisconsin is a grand place to go, Wisconsin being the source of many of the world's wonders. But for those who want to fly fish not too far from Chicago, go up north of Platteville, a bit southwest of Madison, and try the Big and Little Green rivers and Castle Rock and Milville creeks. Or go a bit farther northwest and try the West Fork of the Chippewa.

Any other good spots in the Midwest?

Absolutely. There are superb small streams in the southeastern corner of Minnesota, around the small cities of Red Wing, Wabasha, and Winona. It isn't the easiest fishing in the world; the fish don't leap up to your fly. But they are there, in Hay Creek, the Whitewater River, the Root River as it flows through Forestville State Park, and in Garvin Brook above State Road 14 southeast of Stockton. There are nice midsummer caddis hatches in the mornings and evenings.

Farther north in Minnesota is another kind of wonder—the Boundary Waters Canoe Area. These are lakes, scads of them. On most of them, motorboats are banned, so a bit of effort is required. All of them are teeming with fish, including smallmouth bass. In late May or early June while they're spawning, or in the heat of midsummer (which lasts a whole day or two in northern Minnesota) you can get them with surface bugs.

For the Boundary Waters Canoe Area, the place to go is Ely, Minnesota. There you can rent canoes and other gear, and you can get a permit you'll need if you're going to camp overnight, which you'll want to do to get into the interior lakes. Try paddling north up the Moose River, through a couple of small lakes to Lac La Croix. Locate a weedbed or point of land there and you'll find bass.

Then there's the other side of Lake Michigan. In north-central Michigan is the Au Sable River. Just go to the town of Grayling and look around.

That's good to know. Could there be anyplace to fly fish in Texas?

Sure, and one of the nation's premier fly fishing stores is the Austin Angler, right on Congress Street, the main drag of Austin. The folks there will help you. But if they're not around, you can still go to the Guadalupe River.

Where's that?

Not all that far from Austin, south and west. Trout are stocked in December, and live until it gets too hot. The rest of the year try for bass, mostly largemouth. There are several state parks that offer access.

Well, I'll be. Next you'll tell me I can even fly fish in Southern California.

Indeed you can, and not all that far from the smog and slog of Los Angeles. The West Fork of the San Gabriel has a no-kill, fly fishing-only stretch in the Los Angeles National Forest between the Cogswell Reservoir and the confluence of the North and East forks. It's fishable most of the year. There's also Big Bear Lake, and Bear Creek as it flows out of the lake. In and around the San Gabriel Mountains there's good fishing in several small streams. Also, Big Rock and Little Rock creeks on the northern side of the mountains, and San Antonio Creek on the southern side.

Farther north is the Sacramento River, ignored by fly fishers for many years until lately. But it's getting discovered. Hurry up Interstate 5, north of Redding, to the section below the Shasta Dam. There are superb caddis hatches in the springtime.

Wow! Even in California

Even, believe it or not, in Arizona. East of Phoenix, almost to the New Mexico border, is the Fort Apache Reservation, in which are Christmas Tree Lake and its associated streams, in which are a lovely subspecies known as Apache Trout. It's a threatened species, so you can't keep them, but they're lovely to catch and to behold their shiny gold flanks and olive-green heads. You can keep all the browns you catch. There are some restricted fishing areas, and on some stretches you have to pay a $5 daily fee, which is worth it.

Finally, tell me about some of those great western trout streams.

They're great, all right, but some of them are getting kind of crowded. The upper Missouri, for instance, could use a few years of being ignored. One alternative, because it's even more remote and hasn't been quite as overwhelmed, is the Salmon in Idaho. It's the one also known as the River of No Return. Some of it is kind of rough wading, but head north of Sun Valley and you'll find great fishing and some of the most beautiful scenery in the world.

And here's another tip: There's another Salmon River. This one's in Oregon, not very far from Portland, and has a great fly fishing-only stretch, too.

Wonderful. But I guess I have one more question: Don't you know of some lovely stream, hardly discovered by most fly fishers, where the scenery is tremendous, the ambience peaceful, the water clean and cold, and the fish feisty and plentiful?

Yup. As a matter of fact, we do.

Oh, great. Where is it?

Are you out of your mind?

14.

ENVOI:
A FEW
CLOSING THOUGHTS

Do I now know all the basics?
  Most, but not all.

What's left?
  First of all, the cigars.

Cigars?
  Yes. It's important to know how to light a cigar in mid-stream. It's part of the ethic.

How's that? And what if I don't smoke cigars?
  Our regrets. But even so, it's part of the ethic, which we shall presently explain.

Well, I'm intrigued. Puzzled, but intrigued, so I'll play along for now. How does one light a cigar in midstream?

Place your rod under your arm, extract the cigar from your pocket, unwrap it, and *be sure to put the wrapper in a vest pocket, not in the water.*

Got it. Then what?

Bite off the end, which *can* go in the water, place the cigar firmly in the mouth, and get matches, preferably wooden, out of a pocket high in your vest where you've kept them so they won't get wet.

Makes sense. What's next?

If it's not breezy, just light up. If it's a little breezy, turn downwind and light up.

And if it's very breezy?

Here's an old trick from basic training: Lay the match along the cigar, the match head right on the cigar's end. Then rub the lighting element of the matchbook along the match head, and as soon as it begins to spark, draw on the stogie.

Is that it?

No. Don't put that match in the water, either. Wait a second for it to cool off and put it in that same garbage pocket where you put the wrapper.

Oh, I see. This is really a lesson in streamside etiquette.

You're half right. We're talking about specific fly fishing etiquette, which is related to the specific fly fishing *Weltanschauung.*

Specific fly fishing *what?*

Well, okay. Maybe that was a little much. Let's just say the fly fishing point of view. As we said in the Introduction, there is something of a philosophy involved here, and while we don't want to get too heavy about it, we don't want to ignore it, either.

Okay, how do we start?

With the etiquette. The backpackers, with whom we are somewhat allied, like to say, "Take only pictures; leave only footprints." We don't go quite that far. Sometimes we take fish. But with two exceptions, we leave nothing.

One exception is the cigar tip. What's the other?

The butts. Assuming your cigar has natural leaf wrapper (and if it doesn't, you barely deserve to live, much less fish), you can flip it into the water when you're done.

That's a relief. I wouldn't want to dirty up my vest with old ashes. What about at the other extreme? Is there anything I should be especially careful *not* to drop into the water?

Good question, and the answer is yes. And the specific answer is monofilament.

Oh. You mean leader material, right?

Right. It can wrap around fish. And birds eat it. In fact, birds eat anything, including plastic bags, another item to be especially careful about. Birds will also use monofilament in their nests, which can end up killing them and their young.

I'll remember. But what about the tiny piece of tippet I trim off after tying on my fly?

Ideally, you should even try to catch that and put it in your garbage pocket. But if it falls into the water, it's too small to worry about.

Anything else strictly *verboten*?

Yes. The pull tabs on beer and soda cans. On a really hot day, having a midstream beer is a delight. But if that tab gets into the water, a tiny fish can swim into it, get caught in the middle of it, and grow large on both ends while staying far too slim in the middle.

All that is good to know. What else should one not do?
Shuffle.

What's that?
That's finding a place where there are lots of fish, usually trout, and churning the water with your feet and legs so that they swim about in fear, the better to foul-hook them.

Foul-hook? What's that?
Catching a fish in its gill or along its back or anywhere but in its mouth.

Is that possible?
Sure. In fact, it's inevitable that it will happen to you from time to time. But it's nothing to try for. If there are a lot of fish flailing about in panic, there's a fairly good chance that one will brush up against your hook, and if the angle is right the hook will hold, especially if the hook is barbed.

Aren't all hooks barbed?
Most are. But while we're on the subject of do's and don'ts, here's a positive recommendation: Tamp down your barb.

How?
Take any forceps or pliar-type tool and squeeze it.

Won't I lose some fish that way?
Yes, you will. But you'll also be able more easily to unhook the fish you do catch, making it more likely that they will survive.

I understand that. But who does this shuffling?
Regrettably, some guides do it because they want their cus-

tomers to come back again, and their customers, some of them, only want to catch lots of fish, no matter how.

And that's not what we want to do?

No. We want to catch a lot of fish, but it does matter how. In fact, to a fly fisher, the how matters more than the how many. One great fly fisher and fly fishing philosopher, Robert Traver, whom we have mentioned before, even says that catching too many fish in any single day is something of a drag.

Fly fishing philosopher? How many of those are there?

Were this a perfect world, there would be as many fly fishing philosophers as there are fly fishers. We don't want to get too serious here. Fly fishing is fun. It's a sport and a recreation. But it's a philosophy, too, and the philosophy is part of the fun.

Elaborate a bit. But only a bit.

That's all we intend. First, as we said in the Introduction, there is the creative element—the creation of an illusion. To quote Traver again, "Fly fishing is first of all a combined act of high deceit and low fakery aimed at creating the illusion that a bent pin adorned with assorted fluff is something good to eat."

Continue.

Then there is the aesthetic and natural element.

That's two elements.

No, it's really a combo. Conrad Voss Bark said that fly fishing is both "aesthetic and sensual." Fly fishing presents a unique communication with nature, in part because you have to know something about the stream and its ecology to succeed, and the more you know, the more successful you'll be. Someone once said that while everyone liked a woodland stream, "to an angler it is a community of many forms of life."

You're full of quotes today.

Permit us just one more. Remember when you landed your first fish and you released it and called it "my friend"?

I do.

Well, that shows there's also a communion between the fly fisher and his prey. W. D. Wetherell said that the fly fisher confronts the fish he or she catches with an attitude combining "profound curiosity with deep respect."

Don't other fishermen?

Less, because there is more hardware, more technology intervening. And also because it's easier.

Ah, we're back to deliberately making matters as difficult as possible?

Not really as difficult as possible. Just difficult. Fly fishing is for those who hold that the fun in the race of life is in the running, not just the winning, that existence is its own justification, that a day spent in a stream or a pond with a goal in mind is a joy even if the goal is not achieved, though a greater joy if it is.

I understand all that. But a while ago you said that streamside ethics were only half of the reason you had to teach how to light a cigar in midstream. What's the other half?

Ah, it's related to what we just said. And cigars just happen to be our subjective accessory in the pursuit of contemplative pleasure. You can use something else—a pipe, a beer, singing (not too loud), or any combination of the above—or nothing else at all. For our purposes, though, standing in a cool stream with a mountain range or a meadow nearby, fly rod in hand and cigar in mouth, is the way God meant mankind to live.

FIT TO BE TIED
OR
KNOT AN APPENDIX

You promised we wouldn't have to learn a lot of knots.

And you don't. But it might be helpful to know how to make two more connections.

Which connections?

We figure you don't have to know how to tie backing onto your reel, or the fly line to the backing. The store did that for you when you bought your outfit, and they'll probably hold for years, as long as the line lasts.

And I already know how to tie the fly to the tippet. And with loops, you don't have to know how to tie the tippet to the fly line. So what else do I have to know?

How to tie the loops.

But the leaders and lines *come* with loops tied.

Yes, and the loop in the line is sturdy enough to last for years. But the loop in the leader might break, mightn't it? And you wouldn't want to have to throw away a perfectly good leader just because the loop broke, would you? Especially when you're on the stream and it's the last good leader you've got.

No, I guess not. Okay, how do I make a loop?

By making a loop

You're doing tautologies again.

Not really. Take the tip of your leader (but not now; try this first with thicker stuff, like maybe plastic clothesline) and form a loop by folding it back along the rest of the leader for a few inches. With your thumb and forefinger, hold the main part of the line and the end part, with just a little bit of the tip poking out beneath your thumb.

Like this?

Yup. Now forget about the tip for a few minutes. Take the main part of the leader and make another loop, a bigger one, *under* your thumb and forefinger, and then make a second loop *over* them, overlaying the first loop. Now you have a figure eight, with two loops on its top half and one on its bottom.

That's not so hard. Now what?

Take your single loop, the one under your thumb and forefinger, and wrap it through the double loop twice.

Once, twice.

Now, this next step take a touch of dexterity. Grab the very tip of the end *and* the main part of the leader (or line or whatever you're practicing on) between the fingers of one hand, and the *single loop* between the same fingers of the other hand, and tighten slowly.

Hey, I have a loop.

Specifically, you have the surgeon's loop, or you will as soon as you trim off the tip.

Now I can't think of what other connection I'd have to make, now that I have my backing and my fly line attached and I can reloop my leader if the loop breaks.

But you might want to build onto your leader a bit.

Build?

Right. Every time you change flies, your tippet gets shorter, and you get up toward the heavier, butt part of the leader. And again, maybe it's late in the day and it's the last leader you've got. Or maybe you're using a 3X when you switch to a smaller fly and you don't have a 5X leader but you have some 5X and 4X tippet you can tie onto the butt to improvise a smaller leader.

You can buy just plain tippet?

Sure. You can buy all kinds of monofilament thicknesses and create your own leader. All you have to do is know how to tie a surgeon's knot.

Surgeon's knot, surgeon's loop. Pretty soon I'll be able to perform an appendectomy.

Not on us, you won't. But you will be able to lengthen your tippet simply by paying attention for a few minutes.

Lay on, MacDuff.

Lay on is the trick. Lay the new tippet you're going to attach alongside the leader, overlapping it by about 4 inches.

That's easy.

It's all easy if you just treat this double strand as though it were one single strand. Just make a plain overhand knot by bringing the tippet and the very end of the leader over and through. But don't tighten it.

Why not?

No, this is not a Y knot. This is a surgeon's knot.

Hey, cut the jokes. I'm midknot.

No, it's about three-thirty. Sorry. You don't tighten it because you repeat the step. Just make another overhand knot by bringing the same double strand (the tippet and the very end of the leader) over and through the loop once more.

That's all?

Except for remembering to hold all four ends firmly while you slowly pull the knot tight. Then trim off all the tag ends as close as possible to the knot. But don't cut the knot.

Of course not.

No, we won't teach the coarse knot. This is all you need for now.

A VERY SELECTIVE BIBLIOGRAPHY

Walton, Izaak. *The Compleat Angler*. This is more philosophy than fishing, in the real Socratic method. But it's the start of fly fishing literature. And, of course, a classic.

Hemingway, Ernest. *Big Two-Hearted River*. The cruel truth is that Nick Adams caught his trout with *live* grasshoppers. But he had to eat, and who are we to quibble with a masterpiece?

Traver, Robert. *Trout Magic*. Wonderful writing by a wonderful man.

Wetherell, W. D. *Vermont River*. It's good and it's short.

Rosenbauer, Tom. *The Orvis Fly-fishing Guide*. The best of the standard instruction books.

Maclean, Norman. *A River Runs Through It.* The first sentence is, "In our family, there was no clear line between religion and fly fishing," and it gets better from there.

Yeats, William Butler. *Song of Wandering Aengus.* Now, this is real trout magic.